THE BLIND MASSEUSE

THE BLIND MASSEUSE

A Traveler's Memoir

from Costa Rica

to Cambodia

ALDEN JONES

TERRACE BOOKS

A trade imprint of the University of Wisconsin Press

Terrace Books
A trade imprint of the University of Wisconsin Press
1930 Monroe Street, 3rd Floor
Madison, Wisconsin 53711-2059
uwpress.wisc.edu

3 Henrietta Street
London WC2E 8LU, England
eurospanbookstore.com

Printed in the United States of America

Library of Congress Cataloging-in-Publication Data

Jones, Alden.
The blind masseuse: a traveler's memoir from Costa Rica to Cambodia / Alden Jones.
pages   cm
Includes bibliographical references.
ISBN 978-0-299-29570-7 (cloth: alk. paper)
ISBN 978-0-299-29573-8 (e-book)
1. Jones, Alden—Travel.   2. Travel.   3. Voyages and travels.   I. Title.
G465.J647   2013
910.4—dc23
2013014543

"Lard Is Good for You" originally appeared in *Coffee Journal*, December 1999, and was
reprinted in *Best American Travel Writing 2000*. "The Answer Was No" originally appeared in
Gulf Coast, Summer/Fall 2004, and was named Notable Travel Writing in *Best American
Travel Writing 2005*. "This Is Not a Cruise" originally appeared in *The Smart Set*, Fall 2007.
"The Burmese Dreams Series" originally appeared in *Post Road*, December 2010, and was
named Notable Travel Writing in *Best American Travel Writing 2011*.

This is a work of nonfiction. Some names and identifying details have been changed, and in
some cases chronology has been sparingly condensed or rearranged for the benefit of narrative
clarity.

For
MY PARENTS

and for
KATE

Contents

CONTENTS

THE BLIND MASSEUSE

INTRODUCTION

The Charm of the Unfamiliar

While walking home to Rafael's house, I bumped into a cow. It wasn't too unusual to encounter a cow in a place like La Victoria, Costa Rica; I was in farmland, after all. But because it was pitch black, I didn't understand at first what had happened to me. My belly made contact with something firm, but fleshy, and I bounced lightly backward and stopped. When I aimed my vision at the invisible obstruction, I began to make out the outline of the cow's back and ears and the white spots on her hide.

The cow had wandered out of a nearby enclosure and stopped to rest, or perhaps sleep, in the middle of the dirt road I took home every day. I had been out drinking Imperial beers with my friend Lisa in Turrialba. I'd taken a cab home because buses stopped running at 7:10. It was now around nine, very late. Between the few stray streetlights and the moonlight I could usually make my way to the end of town where I lived with Rafael and his family. Sometimes I tripped on stray rocks or stumbled over roots, but a cow had never been an obstacle on this path, not even in daytime.

The cow was undisturbed. I was calm but I realized I was holding my breath. It had been a shock, being sent backward like that.

I pat-patted the cow in apology, made my way around her, and continued down the path.

Inside the few concrete square houses at the end of town, everyone was fast asleep. The people here were farmers and the children of farmers. I was the only one in town out drinking beers past seven. The sensation of warm bellies meeting remained, and I found myself returning to the moment of bewilderment, the space between being halted in my path and comprehending the presence of the cow. For a few seconds I was in a world that made no sense. If Carolina, the girl who lived in the house I now approached, had made her way down the dark path, she would have likely seen the cow coming. But for me, a girl born in Manhattan and raised in New Jersey who had been in rural Costa Rica only a few months, it was so outside of my experience that it simply did not compute.

The bewilderment lingered—I was savoring it, in fact—and left me with a buzzing feeling in my head. It was a tiny thing, a tiny moment. But I was completely in my body and my life in a way that felt rare and very good.

That buzzing in my head was the feeling of exoticism. It was the delight of having something bizarre or unfamiliar happen, and knowing that, from the point of view of anyone inside those concrete houses I passed, it was absolutely unremarkable. It was bizarre only because of cultural context. It was the split in my own perspective of the world. These moments of absurdity made me feel so alive I almost felt high.

Many travelers seek out this high. We seek out what is different from what we behold in our daily lives, whether it is language, fashion, standards of behavior, architecture, climate, or animal species, because beholding what is different has the quality of being unreal. If our brains resist the realness of something, but this thing is before our eyes, we're accompanied by little sparks of excitement just by moving through the world. While tourists spend their time away from home seeking out the comforts of home, travelers risk—even cultivate—discomfort, because what they want is the thrill of a new perspective. What is it like to reside in a culture where women must cover their arms and legs and still be subject to harassment? What does Nicaraguan *mondongo* taste like? How much guilt can you handle when you compare your comfortable American life to the lives of Burmese terrorized, every day, by their own government?

For most of my life, I have traveled seeking answers to hard questions. I've traveled to understand the human condition in its relativity. I've traveled to learn other languages and to do my best to understand people across cultures. I've also traveled for the high.

Travel was always a part of our family's life, but it was not something we considered glamorous. My father, a golf course architect, traveled all over the United States and internationally, but he was dedicated to being a present parent and cultivated a strong domestic business. As a family, during my childhood, we traveled along the East Coast, visiting my mother's family in North Carolina and my father's in Florida. The places we traveled were too familiar to be exotic.

Exoticism, by definition, is the charm of the unfamiliar. Europe first snagged my attention as the distant but attainable Other when I was fourteen. The difference between the United States and Europe was embodied, I thought, in the design of my high school history textbooks: my U.S. history text, crammed with tales of musket battles and Puritan restraint, was housed in a bland beige cover and decorated with the muted foliage of a Hudson River School painting; my European history text was boldly red and showcased a royal family clad in finery and encircled by tapestries, silver, burning candles, and oil paintings. The deeper into the red text I studied, the more entranced I was by open feuds between royal families, the zeal required to risk one's life laboring on a cathedral, and such bad behavior as blatant looting in the name of religious crusades. I was bright-eyed for the city of Paris and the islands of Italy and Greece. Exoticism often begins—Gustave Flaubert could tell you this—in books. As a teenager I read Sartre for fun (though I did not understand him even in English) and fantasized about the day I would read him in French. I traced the Greek alphabet from the *World Book Encyclopedia* and requested Berlitz tapes for Christmas, imagining that someday the fluency I would acquire from repeating strange phrases would grant me passage to the lands of their origin.

In the beginning it was about language.

Before I entered fifth grade, I was given the choice between Spanish or French. I was entering a new school, and the only person I knew at that intimidating place was Kim Charlton, my nursery school pal. I thought I might prefer French (I had the sense that French was glamorous), but chose Spanish because Kim Charlton had chosen Spanish. This childhood friend unwittingly changed the course of my life, because, as it turned out, Spanish felt like a fun new game, and because I loved it on my tongue, I practiced it, I studied it, I was driven by desire for it to come faster and more fluently out of my own mouth. Unlike Central America—this was the '80s—my parents considered Spain a safe place for a teenaged girl to travel, and they agreed to send me to Spain for a summer of language classes and a homestay. I studied abroad in Seville my junior year of college and dreamed and thought in *castellano*. Then I wanted to go everywhere Spanish was spoken.

Spain was glamorous. I danced sevillanas in a yellow flamenco-style dress, rode on fast trains, and savored frothy café con leche served in weighty white cups. The slang of Seville was enchantingly brash. I was fairly sure *I* was glamorous when I managed this tricky vernacular, and I had a brief but glamorous affair with my Cervantes professor, a handsome womanizer who taught me how to tastefully peel and eat whole-cooked shrimp and ushered me into corner bars normally unpopulated by Americans. The further I got inside the culture of Spain, the closer I came to speaking like a Spaniard, the more I wanted to be at the center.

The exoticist chases this feeling: the sense you are part of the very thing that once excited you for its inaccessibility. After Spain I sought out new foreign charms. But I wanted an experience that was *more* foreign. The charm of the unfamiliar need not always involve glamour; it might be the shock of the unfamiliar, even a scandalized reaction to the unfamiliar. I wanted to go places that were *really* different; I even wanted it to be hard to take. What would it be like, say, to live in isolation on a coffee farm in Costa Rica, in a town where no one spoke English—to put myself in a position of outright alienation? What would I learn about myself, and the human condition? And where else could I test out these questions? How could I find an *in*?

I found there were ways to roam the globe for pay, or at least break even. But there had to be consequences to a life of constant uprooting and disorientation. How long could I live like this? What would I have to give up? Could I remain geographically unmoored and still have a family, children, a career?

Those were the personal questions. But there were also the bigger, moral questions, and these came once I traveled to cultures paved over by colonialism. Was I, this lone American woman, ambassador of the dominant world culture? What were my obligations, if this were the case? Was I a primitivist who idealized other cultures without really seeing them? Was there even something suspicious about my desire to briefly inhabit other cultures?

Is there a right way and a wrong way to travel?

When I graduated college, I signed up as a volunteer for World-Teach and flew straight to Costa Rica to live on Rafael's farm. I taught in La Victoria, where no one spoke English beyond the words I taught them, for a year. Then I spent my life chasing that feeling of bumping into the belly of a cow, the extraordinary-feeling double life of the exoticist.

LARD IS GOOD FOR YOU
(Costa Rica)

I n Costa Rica, I lived on lard and coffee. There was lard in the
bread, in the rice, and in the beans. There was lard in the
cookies, in the imitation Doritos I ate at the school where I
taught; it was coating the potatoes and being used to fry bananas in
the cafeteria. Damaris, the woman I lived with, normally bought
only three food items when she went to the supermarket in the city:
a sack of rice, a sack of beans, and several sticks of *manteca vegetal*
(vegetable shortening). Everything else we ate came off the farm.

The lard came in a fat plastic tube and, unopened, looked like
slice-and-bake cookie dough. For some reason, there were drawings
of clover leaves on the packaging. I watched Damaris fold back the
lard's plastic skin and insert a large metal spoon as she prepared a pot
of rice. She scooped out a generous dollop of the viscous, bone-white
mush and plopped it into the pot.

"Why do you put lard in the rice?" I asked Damaris as she
stirred.

Damaris furrowed her brow slightly as she turned to look at me.
"Lard is good for you," she said.

Out on the farm, Damaris's husband, Rafael, was cutting
broccoli. "Wait until you see this broccoli," he had promised. "It's
beautiful, perfect." Everything Rafael planted grew into something

beautiful and perfect. I helped him work seeds into the soil some-times. He was demanding; he threw work boots at me when he needed my help, and then instructed me on how to bury the seeds and, when the seeds grew into shoots, how to replant them. For broccoli it was three shoots to a hole. He dug the holes by twisting his machete into the ground, and I planted. Dirt pressed under my nails, fast against the quick. This was, unofficially, how I earned my keep. My labor supplemented the checks that Rafael and Damaris received from the government in exchange for my room and board. I did it with pleasure.

Rafael's farm was dominated by coffee bushes, the arabica variety, produced for mass consumption. Banana trees between the coffee bushes were there to provide shade; the bananas that grew on them were a bonus. The other things that Rafael grew—broccoli, chayote, blackberries, sweet lemons—were intended not to be sold, as the coffee was, but to be eaten by him and his family.

"Look at this, Doña," Rafael said, as he entered the kitchen with a full satchel. He opened the satchel on the table and the flawless stalks of broccoli spilled out onto the waxy checkered tablecloth.

"Nice," Damaris murmured approvingly. "Berta!" she called. In a moment her five-year-old daughter scampered into the living room. Berta was precious and wiry and wild, a real gift of a child. Her stick-straight hair hung down over her face. Her feet were bare; she refused to wear socks in the house, and Damaris had given up pushing worn, white socks over her heels just to have Berta peel them off when she wasn't looking. Anyway, most of the children in La Victoria, especially in our neighborhood, ran around barefoot. Their feet withstood the rocky texture of the dirt road that I still had trouble navigating gracefully, even in my hiking boots. "Get me four eggs," Damaris told Berta.

I looked at the broccoli on the table, longing to eat it just like that, still dirt encrusted, hard, and cold. To feel something crunch between my teeth. Before I knew it, Damaris had cleaned and cut the broccoli, thrown it into the frying pan, broken the eggs over it, and dumped the remaining lard—maybe three large spoonfuls—into the pan.

I ate the soggy, eggy broccoli already planning how I would sneak out in the morning with my Swiss Army knife, saw off a fresh stalk, and relish it raw as I hid among the coffee bushes. I would have to do it in secret to keep people from thinking I was crazy. Nobody in La Victoria ate vegetables raw; it just wasn't done. You might as well eat dirt or tree bark. Lard was a component of everything edible, like butter where I grew up, only butter made things taste good, and lard just made things heavy and greasy, as far as my gringa palate could discern.

But I learned. I ate so much lard that I began to crave it; my body seemed to require a daily allotment of it. It was one of two substances that had that effect on me.

The other was coffee. As for the coffee, my addiction had been intact for some time before my arrival. It had little to do with my being in Costa Rica, though it was one of the abstract things that drew me to Costa Rica in the first place, along with the rain forest, the beaches, and a chance to see a three-toed sloth. As it turned out, my job placement found me spending most of my year in the highlands, hours away from the beaches and rain forests I had once associated with Costa Rica. I did see a sloth once, clinging to a tree on the side of the highway. Moss grew in its fur, and when it turned to look at me, it moved as if its batteries were running down.

But coffee—coffee was everywhere I looked. I lived in a town where coffee bushes lined the road, where half of the males over the age of thirteen picked coffee for a living. I loved being surrounded by this drug of mine, seeing it in all of its stages of growth, the red and yellow berries littering the road during coffee-picking season.

Sometimes, during that wet, ripe season, I picked the ready coffee cherries off the bushes and sucked on them like candy, unleashing their juices with the pressures of my teeth. They tasted fresh, the texture fruity but the flavor distinctly caffeinated.

The best berries would be roasted in a nearby city, then exported to countries like the United States. If you've ever read the menu at Starbucks you'll have seen a Costa Rican blend called Tres Rios. If you've ordered this blend, you may have tasted the beans of which I speak, perhaps the very beans I watched grow outside my door, on Rafael's farm, bursting into festive reds and yellows during the rainy season.

Within Costa Rica, you can find choice coffee—Café Américo, Café Britt—in hotels and restaurants that cater to tourists. Off the tourist path, you're more likely to find "inferior" blends, some of them cut with sugar, like Café Maravilla. Brands like Maravilla are made from the lesser beans, some of them green and immature.

But I had trouble telling the difference between those grades of coffee, as well as the flavor of the beans from which they were made. On Rafael's farm, I picked the harder, younger berries before they turned their warm hues and sucked on them as gleefully as I sucked on the red and yellow ones.

Those berries were as delightful as what would become of them.

The lard, however, I could have done without.

I heard voices in my head. There were two of them. Some people have the devil on one shoulder, nudging their id, and the angel on the other, appealing to their superego. I had the tourist and the traveler, two entities that were, in my mind, just as polarized.

On my left shoulder sat the tourist. When it spoke to me, it encouraged me to ditch this dinky town and make a beeline for the beach, where I could stay in a nice hotel with fresh sheets free of that mildew smell. The tourist sometimes wished I could speak English instead of struggling with Spanish all the time, and maybe hang out with a few more gringos. On Thursday nights around ten o'clock, when I was lying on the raised plank that served as my bed, sleepless, the tourist whispered in my ear, "You know, Alden, if you were in the States right now, you could be curled up on the couch watching *ER*."

The traveler sat on my right shoulder, embarrassed that it should have to share a host with someone as crude and culturally insensitive as the tourist. When I was coming home from the city, even when I had enough money to take a cab, the traveler encouraged me to take the bus like everyone else in La Victoria. "You're not a spoiled gringa," the traveler chided me. The traveler reveled in the fact that I lived many kilometers—only the tourist still thought in miles—from any American hotels or restaurants, and it would object to the term American, since Costa Rica was as much a part of America as the United States.

When the tourist watched me being served food fraught with that tasteless, pointless lard, its little voice sounded in my left ear: "No, Alden. Don't eat that. It's just not worth it. It will make you fat, and it sits like cement in your stomach. You would never eat that at home."

Then came the voice of the traveler, the one who wanted me to fit in. "Shut up," it told the tourist. To me it said, "Just do whatever you have to. You're not here to challenge anything, you're here to learn. *You want to be Costa Rican.* So eat the lard, gringa! EAT THE LARD!"

Lard, I ate. I had no choice; it was lard, or starve.

At home there was no coffee. I found this strange, like living on a farm in Idaho and not having potatoes in the cupboard. In the mornings I was served *agua dulce*, a sweet, hot drink made from sugar cane. Damaris used a knife to scrape off bits of what looked like a big block of brown sugar and stirred it into hot water. It looked and tasted like watered-down maple syrup.

"Coffee is bad for the stomach," Damaris explained. "Imagine the pain I had, Alden. The doctor told me coffee has cocaine in it."

I thought for a moment. "Do you mean caffeine?"

"Yes," Damaris corrected herself. "*Cafeina*. So the doctor told me to stop drinking it."

I yearned for coffee, and lived in the one house in La Victoria—on a coffee farm, no less—where coffee was banned. I was a contemporary Ancient Mariner: coffee, coffee, everywhere, and not a drop to drink! There were no restaurants in La Victoria, only a cantina, and Rafael had forbidden me from going there.

He had pointed out the cantina on my first day in town. It was a one-room building with a Coca-Cola sign painted on the wall, and it had swinging doors, like a saloon. "The only women who go there are prostitutes," Rafael had explained to me with a warning stare. He was often very stern with me, as if I were an unruly twelve-year-old, and not a schoolteacher of twenty-two. Then, after a second, Rafael softened and said, "Well, not prostitutes really, just bad women." I doubted they served anything other than beer and guaro, anyway. The men inside were bored looking, always hunched over their drinks, and if they caught sight of me as I walked by, they hissed: "*Macha! Gringa!*" Rafael's warnings were moot; it was clear that the cantina was not the place to go for coffee.

There was nowhere else to buy it either. La Victoria was a very, very small town. There was one road. Everyone swore it would be paved by the time I left; it never was. Along the road there was a church that doubled as a *pulpería* (it sold candy, Coke, batteries, diapers), a nursery school, and an elementary school for grades 1–6.

A woman sold vegetables out of her house. That was it. The high school was in a nearby town called Juan Viñas. Some took the bus to school in Juan Viñas, but high school was optional and many teenagers chose to pick coffee, cut sugar cane, or have babies instead.

My life was at the school. My life was with the kids, teaching them English, and learning Spanish from them. We traded word for word. I liked the arrangement, though the time in between sometimes dragged, and without coffee, I dragged along with it.

Things changed when I met Ana. I was outside on the patio, munching on cookies between class, and she walked up to me just like that.

"You're La Teacher," she observed. I wasn't hard to pick out. I was blonde, and my clothes were different. La Victoria had never had a gringa teacher before so I was somewhat of a celebrity.

"Yes," I said.

"My son, Jason, is in the first grade," she said. Jason . . . dark eyes, quiet in class. I met so many people during my first months in La Victoria, and it was always, somehow, a shock to connect relatives to each other. It was made more difficult by the fact that everyone seemed related. "Why don't you come over to my house after school?" Ana suggested. "Have a little coffee."

Coffee? "Okay," I said. She pointed across the street. "Just go over there and ask for Ana," she said.

Ana lived in the compound next to the church. Jason was an agile soccer player with enormous brown eyes. He was shy, but get him in the school yard with a soccer ball, even a little plastic one, and the kid was in the zone. Ana had those same saucer eyes and black, feathered hair. Their house was one in a row of tiny box-like houses that the government had built for low-income families. I walked through Ana's open door to find her sitting in front of the television, watching a telenovela.

"That Eduardo," she said, shaking her head at the television screen. "He's no good. He cheats on María Luisa and last week he slapped her. He's just like my husband."

"Where's your husband?" I asked, looking around suspiciously. But the only other room in the house, the bedroom, was partitioned off by a thin curtain, and I already knew there was no one home but us.

"He left me," said Ana, and her eyes started to tear. "He's been gone for a year." Just as I was beginning to wonder if I should comfort her, she pushed her tears away with a fist and stood up. "Would you like some coffee, Teacher?"

"If it's not any trouble," I said, attempting a casual shrug.

Ana walked into the kitchen and plugged in the coffeemaker. In my house, a mesh bag that Damaris had once used to make coffee hung on the wall. Powdered coffee was placed inside the bag, boiling water poured through it, and a coffee cup held underneath. Ana was more modern: She had a Mr. Coffee. Ana also had an electric stove, as opposed to the wood-burning stove that Damaris used.

Ana prepared a plate of crackers while the coffee was brewing, slapping margarine on one and then placing another cracker on top, like margarine sandwiches. "Not worth it," whispered Tourist, who had snuck into my left ear. I sighed. When the coffee was ready, Ana poured a big mugful and added three spoonfuls of sugar from the jar on the table.

"My husband is going with another woman now," Ana said, handing me the mug. Like a Pavlovian dog, I felt my heart speed up as I brought the cup to my lips. The coffee was bitter without milk, but full and delicious.

I sipped at my coffee as Ana showed me her photo album, pausing over pictures of her husband, a very young-looking man with a moustache. "He's not the best man," said Ana. "He hit me. He hit Jason. But Jason needs a father, you know."

"It seems like you're better off without him," I offered.

"I don't know," Ana said, shaking her head. It was clear to me that she would take him back in a second.

Suddenly I had a friend. A friend who filled and refilled my coffee cup until my hands shook. I was happy.

I told Rafael and Damaris over dinner. "I went to Ana Solano Coto's house after school," I said. "She's very nice. We had a good chat."

I watched Rafael and Damaris exchange a look and I wondered why they didn't say anything. Finally Rafael said, "Ana is not a good woman." His lips were pulled tight into the agitated grimace he sometimes wore, and I felt chastised, though I didn't know why. I brought my attention back to my rice and beans and left it at that.

Between classes, when I had nothing to do, I hung out in the cafeteria with Doña Ruth, the cook. Doña Ruth was an enormous woman who came to town on the bus. She served up rice and beans for lunch every day, plus mortadela—a mysterious kind of processed meat—or other meat products when the school's budget allowed. Later in the year, I saw an exposé on the news revealing that mortadela was made from horse flesh. They showed footage of skinned horses strung up on meat hooks. The skinned horses were red, and looked strange, as if they were wearing costumes.

"Eat the horse, gringa," Traveler whispered, and I did.

Still, when I watched Doña Ruth scoop such generous helpings of lard into the rice on the stove, the voice of Tourist rang in my head. "Make her stop!" it said. "Tell her she doesn't need to put in that much!"

"She's kind of right about that," conceded Traveler, and I asked Doña Ruth why she put lard in the rice.

Doña Ruth looked at me sideways. "That's how you make rice," she explained simply. After all, she was the professional.

"When I make rice," I said, "I don't add any lard at all. Or just the tiniest bit of oil."

"You can't make rice without lard," Doña Ruth said. "It would get all stuck together."

"That doesn't happen when I make rice," I said.

"You must have a different kind of rice in the United States," said Doña Ruth, and she scooped another spoonful out of the tub, adding it to the pot of beans.

We drank coffee during morning recess. The teachers made it in the school's electric coffeemaker. I helped carry out the tray of coffee cups and the metal sugar container with its lumpy, yellow sugar. I was getting used to drinking coffee with lots of sugar and no milk.

The teachers laughed at me as I drained the last of the coffee pot into my cup.

"Ay, Teacher," said Elsita, the second-grade teacher. "What a *cafetera* you are."

I loved it that they had a word for someone who drinks a lot of coffee.

Miraculously, despite my eating habits, I did not gain weight. I lost weight. Maybe some chemical bond between the caffeine, lard, rice and beans, and occasional chlorophyll molecules made energy-burning more efficient, I considered. Or perhaps food was beginning to lose its appeal. I couldn't take all the lard-ridden food; though I craved it, I became full far more quickly than I normally did. And I was becoming downright skinny.

I learned that in Costa Rica, one's appearance was an open topic for conversation. If you looked pale one day, several people might grimace and say, "*Ay*, Teacher, you look really pale today." At the first signs of weight gain you would be called *gorda*, fat girl. If you were fat enough, Gorda might become your permanent name, as Teacher had become mine. Suddenly, the first time in my life, I was becoming *flaca*, skinny girl. Ana soon commented on my newer, bonier self.

"Teacher," she said. "You're wasting away! Is Damaris feeding you?"

"Rice and beans, every day," I told her.

What I didn't tell her was that Damaris and Rafael had officially given me a talking-to about my visits to Ana's. They didn't like Ana—not one bit. She wore Spandex shorts, for one thing. Also, Rafael was friends with Ana's husband, and thought the breakup had been Ana's fault.

"She drove him away," Rafael said. "She was a bad wife."

"But Ana said her husband used to hit her, and their son," I objected.

Rafael looked at me blankly. "You have to teach them somehow," he said.

I still snuck over to Ana's house after school, on the sly, like a teenager with an undesirable boyfriend. Ana was my best friend. She always gave me coffee and filled me in on the telenovela that was her life.

In March, there was big news. "The woman!" Ana said, slamming her hand down on the arm of the fake leather couch. "Did you hear about the woman?"

"What woman?" I asked, feigning innocence; Ana was not the only gossip in La Victoria, and I'd heard a small buzz about Ana's husband having a girlfriend.

"That harlot, the one my husband is seeing. She's having a baby! She's already big!" Ana started to cry, plump tears sliding onto her hot pink T-shirt. The T-shirt was tight, and I thought to myself, Rafael would have something to say about that shirt.

I put my arm around Ana and let her cry like that for a while.

"He's a jerk," I assured her. "You're better off without him."

My words never seemed to comfort Ana, though she did seem happy to have someone around to listen to her. Some people in town had lost patience with Ana's endless lamentations about a guy who wasn't worth missing.

"He's not a good fellow," the first-grade teacher told me when I inquired about him. "He left Ana—she's a handful anyway, always complaining—and now he's back in the house he grew up in, living with his mother. Twenty-nine years old and he's still being taken care of by his *mamá*!"

I never met Ana's husband, but I saw "the woman" at school. She wasn't as pretty as Ana. She had buck teeth and hacked-off bangs. Her first daughter—I didn't ask who the father was—came to kindergarten in a cute blue jumper. The woman picked her daughter up at the school every day at noon, and soon I noticed that her belly was growing round.

One day, after he got home from work, Rafael entered the house wearing a huge smile and requested coffee.

"Please, Doña," he begged Damaris. "Could you make some coffee? Just a little coffee?" He whined like a child and flirted with Damaris until she giggled, flattered by the attention, and headed toward the kitchen. I was shocked. I hadn't realized that Rafael still had an appetite for coffee, or that Damaris kept a stash of Café Maravilla on the top shelf of the cupboard. She put a pot of water on to boil and spooned powdered coffee into the sack on the wall.

"Would you like some?" she asked me. "Oh, yes, I *love* coffee," I gushed. Then she yelled into the bedroom, "Berta? Karol? *Café?*"

"Sí," called out Berta and her seven-year-old sister, Karol, in enthusiastic unison, from behind the curtain.

Damaris served me and Karol our coffee in heavy glass mugs, with several spoonfuls of sugar and powdered milk. Though Karol was a healthy weight, the kindergarten teacher had designated Berta Too Skinny (*¡flaquita flaquita!*), and the government provided powdered milk to help fatten her up. With the milk, the coffee tasted like hot, melted ice cream. Rafael received his mug and slapped Damaris on the thigh in thanks.

Berta got her coffee in a bottle. She drank it with childish sucking sounds.

"Do you like coffee, Berta?" I asked her.

"Mmmmpg," she said through the nipple, her eyes already buggy.

A few days later, Dave, my North American director, came to visit me in town. He observed my classes and offered feedback.

"Let's show my boss how smart we are, shall we?" I urged my second graders.

Dave sat in the back of the classroom as the kids and I went through the alphabet, shouting out the words we had learned.

"What are some words that start with *s*?"

"Sun! Sit down! Stomp your feet!"

"'Stomp your feet'?" Dave said after class. "I'm impressed." I was proud, and grateful that he had observed my second graders. He would have been less impressed by the spitballs flying in my third-grade class.

"Are there any problems I should know about?" he asked.

"I'm not having any at the moment," I said. I had already told him about the constant precautions against catching lice. So far my hair was still nit-free. "But my five-year-old host sister drinks coffee out of a baby bottle."

"Kids all over the country drink coffee," he said. "It's available, it always has been. No one worries about it stunting their growth."

"And then there's the lard thing," I said.

Dave smiled as if he was used to gringas complaining about the lard content of the Costa Rican diet. He was, of course. There were over seventy volunteers in the country at the time, doing what I was doing, and I was not the only one with a tourist on my shoulder.

We were sitting at the school, outside the office. Dave stood out dramatically in the town, even more dramatically than I did, because of his height. He was over six feet tall, and, by Costa Rican standards, blond, though in the States his hair would be called light brown. You could spot his blue eyes from sixty meters away. People—especially women—were staring at him. Some even walked out of their houses to get a better view.

"The lard thing," he said. "Ah, *manteca*. Years ago in Costa Rica, few people could afford to eat meat. Most lived on rice and beans. The thing is, you need a little fat in your diet, just like you need protein and carbohydrates, and there is no fat in rice and beans. So the government advised everyone to start using *manteca*."

"People eat meat now," I observed.

"Lard has become a staple in the Costa Rican diet. Just like coffee." Dave smiled. "So you see, Alden," he said, "lard is good for you. Anyway"—he squeezed my shoulder—"you look like you could use a little meat on your bones."

The pregnant woman—I still did not know her name—walked by the schoolyard. She was not shy; she craned her neck to stare at us as she passed.

"Look," I said, nodding my head in her direction. "That's the woman who's pregnant with my friend Ana's husband's child. But Ana's husband doesn't live with either of them. He lives with his mother."

My director laughed at me. "You're becoming quite the *chismosa*," he said. The girl who gossips. In a word, I felt like I was becoming one of them—the women of La Victoria.

The girlfriend had her baby, another girl.

"He didn't even go with her to the hospital," said Ana. She seemed conflicted about this. She smiled, as if gloating; then her brow wrinkled and her gaze fell, as if she felt the indignation of single mothers around the world.

I was teaching animals that week. In my first-grade class, I held up a picture of a dog.

"Dog," I said. The kids repeated the new word.

I barked. The kids cracked up, then barked. "Who wants to be a dog?" I asked.

Hyperactive Rosa Elena was soon on all fours, barking and howling, crawling up to her classmates and nipping at their heels. Soon twenty-five first graders were laughing, screaming, and pretending to be dogs. Any minute the fourth-grade teacher would appear in the doorway and glare at the kids until they shut up, which would be never, once they started.

Ricardo's shrill voice cut through the din. "Look," he said, pointing outside the classroom door, "it's the Red Cross!"

A wave of gasps passed through the room. I looked out the door and there it was, the Red Cross van, bouncing over the rocky road, heading east. The Red Cross only came when something terrible was happening. This was the first time I'd even seen it; until now, I'd only heard about it in the context of horror stories, like the time Rafael told me, "Gemelo's brother got run over by a tractor and the Red Cross had to come."

Ana's son, Jason, sat in the back row. He was so quiet, so obedient and sweet. All the quiet kids got stuck in the back. Jason sat at his desk, staring at me attentively, not knowing that down the road, his twenty-nine-year-old father was having a heart attack.

The doctor said it was the lard," Damaris explained later. "It clogged up his heart."

Word spread like wildfire through the town. Ana's husband had just dropped to the ground while picking tomatoes. The closest phone was in the center of town, and by the time the Red Cross arrived, he was dead.

"He was so young," I said.

"So now we're supposed to stop putting so much lard in our food." Damaris suddenly looked away. Her eyes turned pink. "Just imagine—I didn't know it, but I was killing my husband! My food could have killed him!" She looked at me with disbelief.

"Poor Ana," I said. It was the wrong thing to say. Damaris and Rafael wouldn't talk about her. They both went silent.

"She's better off without him," the teachers in school whispered.

Ana cried after her husband died, but she said it was for Jason, and not for herself. "Jason needs a father," she said. She put a hand on her cheek in distress. "I'm working on getting him a new one," she said, a strangely out-of-place tone of mischief in her voice. "There's a guy in Juan Viñas who thinks I'm pretty."

The gossip at Ana's house took a turn, and from then on, it was Ana telling me about the new men in her life. I listened attentively and sipped at the coffee she made me. The more I listened, the more coffee I drank. I walked home with shaking, sweating hands and a buzz in my head. I avoided telling Damaris and Rafael where I had been. "*Paseando*," I told them—just passing around. And I sat down with them for a lard-reduced meal.

A NORMAL AMERICAN LIFE
(New York)

The worst blizzard of the decade hit days after I moved to New York from the sunny climes of Costa Rica. Elevators all over the city were out. Snowplows growled through the streets like tanks and piled snow on top of the cars parked along the curb; the city became a maze of tunnels with five-foot walls of packed snow.

I had just signed a lease with my college boyfriend, David. We'd been living in New York for exactly three days when it was buried in white. When the snow stopped falling, we walked twenty blocks uptown to the movie theater in parkas and rubber boots, just to have something to do. The voice of the city was muffled and our footsteps echoed off the snow. We joined the parade of pedestrians walking in the middle of streets, occasionally stepping aside for a taxi coasting down Broadway or Sixth Avenue.

I was born in this city, but the week I moved back, New York was the most exotic place in the world. I was perpetually puzzled, not only by the weather and the fact that human beings had settled in such a climate, but by the hustle, the fact that no one seemed to possess the time or good nature to smile at a stranger, the availability of quality goods (like well-made shoes and nail polish), and the sheer variety of simple things. Why did one supermarket carry seven brands of cheddar cheese? Who needed that much choice? In La Victoria, no one had more than they needed, and if something cost more than it should, you simply didn't purchase it. Life was need based, not choice based, and I had grown accustomed to that way of life. I never saw Rafael happier than the day he walked in the door and announced he had purchased a washing machine so Damaris would not have to spend all morning hand-scrubbing clothes with a big blue bar of soap. At the school where I taught, we had chalk and erasers and worn, torn books and few other materials. Fifth- and sixth-grade boys hoed cilantro behind the school building so we would have something to flavor our lunchtime rice and beans. Now I was back among my friends from college, some of whom paid six hundred dollars for a pair of pants. Sometimes, as when I stood in a department store mentally calculating the cost of the clothes on the racks that stretched into infinity, I felt, literally, cold.

The WorldTeach directors had warned the volunteers that this might happen.

"I think I'm suffering from Reverse Culture Shock," I told David.

"Sounds bad," David said. He was the mellowest, warmest person I knew. Nothing fazed him, including the fact that I was fazed by something as standard to him as the cereal aisle in the grocery store. We had been friends since our freshman year in college, periodically veering into coupledom and then back to friendship and then back again. Finally, when I returned from Costa Rica, we decided to try out life together. When the snow began to melt and the electricity was restored, we bought used furniture and groceries and claimed New York as home. Soon enough, everything in front of me appeared normal again.

I returned to New York to live the normal American life I had always expected to live. I began a graduate program in creative writing at

New York University and found part-time work as a receptionist. David temped at an advertising agency and found acting gigs here and there. I wrote short stories; took literature courses on such topics as Melville, Hawthorne, and Whitman; and devoured, in large quantities, the foods I had missed eating while in Costa Rica.

Oh, *Diós santo*, the food! On Sundays I strolled to University Place for doughy bagels plastered with garlic, salt, and poppy seeds, a tub of whipped cream cheese, and the *New York Times*, and David and I read the morning away in the luxury of just-toasted, teeth-sinking New York bagels. I ate sushi without a thought to cholera. And coffee—coffee was everywhere. Coffee was available at the deli, where it would be made from cheap grounds, but freshly brewed; coffee with steamed milk was accompanied by a good magazine at News; good coffee with whipped cream and caramel drizzle was a reliable indulgence at Starbucks. There was American coffee, espresso, French press, iced, Thai, Turkish, all within blocks of my apartment. David and I had a basic espresso maker and a milk frother, so I even had good coffee at home. Our shower had hot water, *always*. These simple luxuries were beyond measure.

At the office and in my graduate classes, I was surrounded by people who could converse endlessly about books. After a year talking about little beyond *los chiquitos*—the children I was teaching—and living with a family who didn't know there was even such a thing as graduate school for writing, much less understand why I would want to keep going to school beyond getting a nuts-and-bolts education that would earn me a living (in their mind, I was a teacher; I already had a good job), I was living exactly the life I thought I wanted to live. I tucked away my loose sundresses and farm-practical shoes and returned to jeans and tight shirts and boots with a heel, drank gin and tonics at bars that didn't have crowds until 10:00 p.m., and spent hours writing and reading at cafés and grazing my fingers along spines at bookstores.

I was happy. David and I were doing a good job of living in the moment; neither of us had any intention of settling down in any permanent way—there was still too much to do. At school, my job, and socially, I could have asked for little more. At the same time, a few things nagged at me and it felt like actual ache.

I missed speaking Spanish. Yes, there were plenty of Spanish-speaking New Yorkers. I had daily conversations with Luis, from Guatemala, who stood outside the garage next door to my building every morning, and found myself hanging out with the service staff at more than one party. One of my best friends from college, Lizanne, was from Puerto Rico; she tolerated my Spanish. But this spotty conversing wasn't the same as being divorced from one's native tongue, of *being* in another language. And, not surprisingly, as days in the office began to blend together, I felt the familiar urge to escape my quotidian vistas.

Luckily for me, grad school came with summer vacation, and I had an idea for a summer job.

When I was in high school, I'd gone on a trip to Spain with a company called Putney Student Travel. Putney was owned and run by two brothers, Jeffery and Peter Shumlin, whose parents founded the company fifty years prior. It was operated out of a barn in Vermont. When I arrived at JFK at sixteen years old to travel abroad by myself for the first time, Jeff was there to see us off. He was in his early twenties then, tall and slim and handsome with bright blue eyes and a nonchalant traveler-style fashion, and he had handed us each a piece of paper, a short typed essay, the title of which was "The Tourist vs. the Traveler."

"This is the Putney philosophy," Jeff had said. "At Putney we are travelers, not tourists." This was the first time I had considered such a distinction. I considered it a good mission to get behind. I applied for a leadership position. The jobs were competitive, and you had to prove fluency, leadership experience, time abroad, and a general good attitude.

I walked to the apartment on Eighth Street where Putney directors cross-examined prospective leaders. When the door opened, Jeff was on the other side.

"So you want to go back!" Jeff said. He gave me a hug. He interviewed me in Spanish and English, and it felt like old friends catching up, with an edge of evaluation.

When I left, feeling excited, the light brightened Eighth Street in a way it hadn't before. Instead of beelining toward my next destination I found myself slowing down and taking it all in. I entered a pet store, just because I had never been in a New York pet store before. When I exited ten minutes later I carried with me a plastic bag containing water and a flamboyant blue betta fish, a small round bowl, colored pebbles, and a canister of shrimp meal pellets.

David thought the fish was as beautiful as I did. He leaned his guitar against the futon and joined me at the kitchen table to admire our new pet. He pushed his long, brown hair behind his ear.

"What should we name him?" he asked.

Betta fish like to be alone. If you put two betta fish in a bowl together, they will fight until one of them dies. If you hold a mirror up to a lone betta, he will go into a frenzy trying to attack his reflection. They are sometimes called Siamese fighting fish.

"Well, he is an isolationist and an individualist," I said.

"Like the main character in an existential novel," David said. We named him Meursault, for the protagonist of Camus's *The Stranger*. We observed Meursault in his bowl, suspended, unmoving, in the water. The blue of his scales was electric. I wiggled a finger in front of him. His exuberant tail, fringed in deep red, rippled in anger.

"So," I said to David, "will you take care of Meursault if I spend five weeks in Spain?"

David, too, was an individualist and a free spirit; he thought people should do what they wanted to do. He obligingly took in my mail for me, paid my bills with the checks I'd prepared for him, sprinkled shrimp meal into the mouth of Meursault's bowl, and went on with his New York life while I traveled from the north coast to the south coast of Spain, teaching Spanish to American high school students with my coleader and new best friend, Aaron.

Aaron had just graduated from Amherst College. He had close-cropped brown hair, an easy smile, and freckles. We liked each other, in a "friends" kind of way, the minute we met in the airport. He was ambitious and had a mind for business, but he also had a plan: he was going to travel as much as he could for the first few years after college, and after this designated period his career (which, ideally, would include a good deal of travel) would get his laser-focus. We valued a similar balance between ambition/hard work and pleasure/enjoying life. Leading an educational, language-based trip was the perfect embodiment of that balance.

Aaron taught our students how to play rugby on the beaches of Luarca, and he taught me how to drive stick when the students spent a week in private homes in León. We coerced our high schoolers into speaking only Spanish, especially at the dinner table, and we ran language drills twice a day. The rest of the time we rode horses, hiked mountains, looked at art, took photographs, and shared picnics of fresh fruit, bakery bread, and jamón Serrano and cheese wrapped in butcher paper. There were the inevitable discipline issues, and we were exhausted most of the time, but if Putney had called to double the length of the trip I would have been elated.

"How can we make this our job forever?" I asked Aaron, as I shifted gears and pulled our diminutive European car down a narrow road into a hamlet outside of León. Our bellies were full of octopus and *patatas bravas* and Rioja wine.

"We should definitely do it again," he said.

When the summer ended, Aaron flew off to Bolivia to spend the year teaching at an American school in Cochabamba. I returned to New York and found myself in an instant funk. All of a sudden no one needed me, and school didn't start for a month; I had no purpose. David officially despised his temp job, which had become semi-permanent with none of the benefits of a full-time job, but he scoffed at my suggestions that he get more aggressive about pursuing acting gigs. The grind was getting to him, and I was frustrated with his inability to figure out an alternate career route.

"Maybe L.A. is the answer," he said.

"L.A. is not *my* answer," I said. David and I loved each other with a depth that sometimes quarantined us from other people. But whether we were on the same path to happiness was unclear.

Meursault sat on the kitchen table, floating serene in his bowl. In eighteenth-century Siam, kings collected betta fish and bred them for the most brilliant colors and to fight each other to the death in gambling matches. How much of Meursault's instinct to be alone was natural, and how much had his true instincts been artificialized?

When I waggled my finger near the lip of Meursault's bowl, his body leapt in a sudden jerk against the surface of the water. I admired Meursault's spirit. His independence I admired in an anthropomorphizing kind of way. His ability to remain content in one place for months on end, however, I did not relate to at all.

But it was time to get a real job, and when fall came, I secured a dream job that made my New York life regain its shine. It was an entry-level position at a top book publishing company a few short blocks from my apartment.

My desk was off the main hall of the fourth floor, crammed next to the printer. I had a rolly desk chair and a view of bookshelves filled floor-to-ceiling with the company's latest releases. A ladder was stationed there at all times, and I often climbed it to reach books on upper shelves. On Mondays, the floor was slick with wax and the air was thick with the smell of exterminator fluid. Through a window fitted with blinds that were often left up, I could see into my boss's office. He was a kind and instructive boss, and the only thing I could complain about was my skimpy paycheck; but I worked in book publishing, not banking, and the payoff was free books, smart company, and knowing I was doing my part to put something good into the world.

I was ecstatic to have my own desk. While I had been in Costa Rica, my friends from college wrote me letters about their in-boxes being endlessly full and bosses who asked them to redraft letters four or five times. They spoke of these things as if they were a drag. But reading these letters while I stared off at the cornstalks and the muddy puddles on the sugar cane–littered dirt road, sipping my recess coffee, I fantasized about an in-box filled with things that needed to get done. *I* wanted to draft and redraft letters to industry professionals and print them out on crisp letterhead and carry them to the postage meter and then return to my desk for the next task. Now I had that desk. It was understood that—as long as I put in my time in doing the busy work of faxing, photocopying, addressing mailing labels, and entering royalty statements—I would eventually be sitting at my boss's desk, or another desk like it.

A few days a week, I took the elevator down to the ground floor and escaped the building for a coffee break. It was an unwritten rule that, in addition to one's lunch hour, "running out for a coffee" was an acceptable interruption to the workday. When I emerged into the air of New York, I felt free and relieved, and when I returned with my hot latte and a cleared head, I was ready to face my in-box once again.

Aside from the skimpy paycheck, my job had one big problem. The problem was my boss's desk.

The problem with my boss's desk was not the view itself. He looked out over the pretty, petite park of Union Square. There was sky in the window, and in the winter, snowflakes swirled on the other side of the glass. My boss, too, had a wall of books to admire whenever he glanced up from his work.

The problem was the fact that he had been looking at the same view, fifty weeks a year, for six years. The three years before that, his view had been the view from my desk, which was a view of the desk that would eventually become his desk.

"I'm not sure I'm built for this, the nine-to-five, 401(k), fifty weeks a year thing," I admitted to David.

"Why don't you quit?" David asked. He did not understand why someone would work a job she didn't love if she didn't have to. He disliked working in an office, but he felt he had no choice. I was attending my graduate program on a tuition scholarship and also received a monthly stipend. I had been doing fine before this with a part-time job, something I could quit in order to gallivant abroad without inconveniencing anyone. But I had been at this job for only six months, and it seemed rather flaky to throw in the towel.

"What am I going to do, then?" I asked. "Just keep getting jobs and quitting them when I don't like them anymore? That's no way to build a career."

"What about another Putney trip?" David asked.

Of course, this was something I had considered. "I would quit my job to lead a trip," I said, "if the trip is Australia." This was not the answer to a career. You couldn't lead Putney trips year-round, and you couldn't lead them forever.

But the trip to Australia, New Zealand, and Fiji was, among Putney leaders, the holy grail. Unlike Spain, it had no academic content. It was a reward. It was pure frivolous fun paired with athleticism: skiing in New Zealand, sailing in the Whitsunday Islands, and snorkeling and lying in the sun in Fiji. In Spain, when Aaron and I felt pleased with ourselves for being frugal with company money or taking our students on a particularly successful excursion, we would say to each other, "We're totally getting Australia." It was a trip neither of us could have afforded on our own, and it attracted notoriously difficult teens, but if we were getting *paid* . . .

For now, I filed papers. I enjoyed my free books. I tried to ignore the rising dread that increased each time the radio alarm brought me back to waking life.

I am doing something good, I told myself as I entered royalty statements, filed correspondence, and photocopied contracts. I was always aware that I was part of an important machine. But when I read an article about a photographer in Juárez who installed a police radio into his car so he could get to crime scenes to photograph murdered factory workers before their stories disappeared, I couldn't convince myself that what I did on a day-to-day basis was truly important.

I noted that I never faced this particular doubt when I was teaching.

Fantasies about teaching brought to mind an appealing phrase: academic calendar.

One morning, I left the office and walked to the place on Eleventh Street for a latte and my favorite bagel. When I returned, my boss appeared to be in a bad mood. He wouldn't meet my eye until the afternoon, when he bent around the doorframe and said, "Alden, could you come in here for a moment?"

It was obvious that my boss didn't enjoy the "management" part of his job, so I supposed he was mad at me in equal parts for whatever I had done and the fact that I'd required him to call me into the office.

I sat in the chair that faced his desk. "I know people go out for coffee sometimes—I do it—but we really shouldn't. And you've been going to that place that's several blocks away."

He was right; I shouldn't be leaving the office for twenty-minute stretches. I should get my coffee from the coffee shop next door to our office, as most people did, even though it was usually burnt and too strong. I had remorse.

"I'm sorry," I told him. "I won't go that far anymore."

"No," he said. "I'm saying you shouldn't go out for coffee anymore."

I blinked, and waited for a change in his face, but the brow remained knit with the stress of confrontation. Did he just tell me I was not allowed to go out for coffee? Everybody in the office went out for coffee! It was an office worker's *right*! He did it all the time!

"I won't go out for coffee anymore either," he lied. It wasn't but a few days before I saw him sneak out with his coat over his arm and return with his coat awkwardly draped over his hand, creating a suspiciously cup-sized lump.

This put me over the edge. You can put me in an office, but you cannot put me in an office and tell me I'm the only one in it who is not allowed to go out for coffee.

Not long after that, I got a phone call from Jeff at Putney Student Travel.

"How would you and Aaron feel about leading a trip to Australia, New Zealand, and Fiji?" he asked.

I quit my job.

This was around the time Meursault began to jump clean out of his bowl. It started one day when I rubbed shrimp meal between my fingers over the surface of the water. The motion lured him to the top of the bowl, and before I saw him wind up he hurled his bright blue body up and out of the water, lunging toward my finger.

"David!" I said. "Come look!" David and I took turns wiggling fingers over the bowl and provoking Meursault to jump. Meursault performed this trick for several months. A few times, he jumped so vigorously he landed on the table. One day, he jumped out of his bowl when no one was there to scoop him up and return him to the safety of liquid. That was the end of Meursault. I always wondered if he was trying to escape something I'd always assumed felt safe to him.

In the last year of my graduate program, I taught a section of undergraduate creative writing, and imagined what it would be like to do this, to teach college, to walk into a room every day and talk to smart young people about things I cared about. Aaron and I went to Australia, New Zealand, and Fiji to ski the Tasman glacier, sail with dolphins, snorkel in clear water off the Great Barrier Reef, and try to prevent the couple of delinquents in the group from lighting things on fire. Then I dealt with what it meant to finish a graduate program with no job lined up in one of the most expensive cities in the world. I decided to live for a year or two in Vermont, where I could rent a country house with a woodstove and deer in the backyard for next to nothing and work part time in the Putney barn during the winter, answering phones, doing office work, and traveling abroad to do programming. David decided his fate awaited him in Los Angeles, and, bittersweet, we parted ways.

But the very first thing I did after I quit my first and last nine-to-five job—what I did after I shut my apartment door behind me, kicked off my office shoes for good, flipped open my laptop, and connected to my dial-up Internet—was book a ticket to Cochabamba, Bolivia.

COKE IS IT
(Bolivia)

In Bolivia, I was seduced by the hobble-skirt bottle. I had never
been one to drink Coke in a foreign country—it was just too
American—and during my first days in Bolivia, I adhered to
the local brews. I chewed coca leaves and drank maté through a short
metal straw, trying not to suck the leaves into my mouth along with
the liquid. I did what I could to fit in: I wore long sleeves, even in
the heat; I spoke only Spanish, of course; I learned to respect the fact
that the *cholitas*, the Aymara and Quechua women I passed on the
street, wanted little to do with me, a white foreigner. But when I
got sick, as Americans in Bolivia did, it was the most American of all
American things that I turned to: the fizz and sting of Coca-Cola.

But I'm already making excuses. The truth is I turned to Coke
before I got sick. I turned to it like a tourist, because it was easy,
familiar, and always so cold. I was vulnerable to what felt good.

I generally found caffeine in vehicles other than coffee to be a
disappointment. My mind was on coffee when Aaron roused me
from a rough night's sleep on my first morning in Bolivia by placing
his extra set of house keys on the side table next to my bed in the
guest room. Aaron worked during the weekdays while I was visiting.
He had booked us a trip to Sucre for the weekend, but the days before
and afterward I was on my own in the city. I was more than happy to

have the opportunity to get lost in my head on the streets of Cochabamba. The sounds of Spanish and the smells of the unfamiliar and the confusion I expected to face when navigating the streets—these things would reset my brain after all those months getting comfortable as a New Yorker. I was back in the bigness of the rest of the world.

"Where's the best coffee in town?" I asked Aaron.

Aaron and I had drunk many a café con leche in Spain, and I expected an easy reply. Instead Aaron said, "Hm, that's going to be tough. The land is mostly used to grow coca. If you find coffee at all, it will probably be instant."

I opened one eye and looked at him skeptically.

"That doesn't make any sense," I said. Cochabamba was a city. Cities had coffee shops, or at least restaurants where coffee was brewed.

Aaron smiled, wished me luck, and left to catch his bus to school. I slept off my jet lag. In the late morning I put on my favorite travel dress, a crêpey, wrinkle-proof spaghetti-strapped dress with a brown, cream, and blue pattern, and covered my arms with a thin denim button-down shirt. It was too hot for sleeves even at ten in the morning, but obscuring my skin was what I expected to do to offset the long blonde hair and the fact that I was a young, foreign woman moving through the world alone.

On my first day in a new place, I like to be without an agenda, to wander and get a sense of my surroundings. I meandered down the narrow, rubbled streets of Aaron's neighborhood, waiting for men to call "*macha! Hola, gringuita!*" as they would have in Costa Rica. But no men did. A man in a farmer's shirt passed me closely on the sidewalk; when his shoulder collided with mine, I said *perdón*, and even then he did not meet my eye. Sweat sank into the back of my dress, where my backpack bumped to the rhythm of my steps. I considered stripping off my sleeves, but even if they were ignoring me, would the people around me have a bad opinion of too much bare flesh? Above all, I did not want to be the American whose ethnocentric habits offended.

Cochabamba that day was decorated by the metal grilles of closed businesses. I wandered countless blocks; the city, midday in the middle of the week, was dead. Aaron hadn't mentioned that everything would be closed. Eventually I found an open corner store that would accept my fifty-colombianos bill and plucked a pack of cheddar cheese Combos (I was desperate) from a spinning metal rack.

"Do you know where I can get a cup of coffee?" I asked the man behind the counter. He shook his head, mumbled, and grazed me with his eyes. It appeared he couldn't wait to have me out of his store. I crossed the street, leaned against the concrete wall, and tore open the plastic Combos wrapper. A group of three *cholitas* in bowler hats and wide skirts looked through me as they passed, forcing me closer to the wall. It was the gesture of high school girls snubbing an underclass misfit. My adventure, so far, was tinged with the homesick feeling of knowing I was somewhere I didn't belong. As I bit through the salty shell of a Combo, I noticed a scrawl of graffiti on the wall that confirmed this feeling: *YANQUI*, it said, *GO HOME.*

There was a lot I didn't know about what was going on in Bolivia.

Any budding academic can tell you that deliberately placing oneself in a position of not-knowing, and to then go about finding out what you don't know, can be a fulfilling pursuit, and the disorientation itself, the early stages of figuring out what you didn't know that you wanted to know, was as exciting as the eventual discoveries. This was one of the reasons I traveled. I wasn't like my friend Tim, who devoured history books and novels about a country before he visited; though I often wondered why I wasn't as inquisitive as he was, I preferred to go in more or less blind, become curious about things as I observed them, and read the books when I got home. But sometimes, this approach made me feel ignorant. Because sometimes I was.

The research I'd done before jumping on the plane was practical. I educated myself on the climate so I could select the proper clothes. The books said to beware of altitude sickness if you were flying into La Paz (I was); they said that if you didn't adjust slowly your heart may feel like it was beating out of your chest and you may feel dizzy and short of breath (I did). The Bolivian cure for that, the books said, was tea made from coca leaves. But these leaves, which had been a staple of Andean culture since pre-Colombian times, were under attack from the US Drug Enforcement Administration because they were the source of the active ingredient in cocaine, which Americans had a little problem with. So it wasn't like you could just throw a bunch of coca leaves in your travel pack.

I knew from my reading there was strife around the coca plant, and that the DEA was universally considered the villain. While the DEA rationalized that eliminating the cultivation of coca leaves might slow the flow of cocaine to the north, it didn't take into account the fact that Bolivian farmers depended on coca for their livelihoods, or that Bolivians themselves didn't have the nationwide cocaine problem the United States had accomplished. First the US government offered financial incentives to the Bolivian government, then threatened to cut off funding if coca continued to thrive. The result was massive crackdowns on Bolivian farmers. According to Law 1008, the agreement between the United States and Bolivia, eradications were not supposed to be forceful, but violence and death were regular events. Many people—many farmers who had been around coca all their lives—were imprisoned. On US soil, not much changed, but for all appearances, the DEA was "doing something about it." In Bolivia, the people rebelled, including an outspoken congressman named Evo Morales, who criticized both the United States for its interference and the Bolivian government for bending over for the United States.

The night I arrived, Aaron put water on to boil and I opened Aaron's cupboard looking for teacups. I'd been surprised to see a bag of coca leaves sitting innocently next to a box of manzanilla tea. It gave me an excited illicit shiver.

"Aren't these illegal?" I asked.

"Sure," Aaron said, "but everyone chews them. Try some." He showed me how to push leaves to the back of my cheek. I gnashed my teeth and waited for a buzz, but I found the experience disappointing; stems pushed into my gums and I had to fight the urge to swallow the entire lump of leaves.

"They're not that exciting," I said. I spit them out and we drank maté out of Aaron's metal cups instead.

Around coca I knew there was strife. But I was ignorant of the water problems.

I knew water was an issue for people like me, of course. I knew that I couldn't drink tap water or anything with ice cubes in it. I couldn't trust anything from the street, or anything that didn't fit the three *p*'s: packaged, peeled, or piping hot. When I reached for a glass in the drying rack to pour myself a glass of water before bed, Aaron snatched it from my hand, shook his head, and returned it to its place on the rack.

"No way, gringa. There are water droplets all over this glass," he said. "You can't drink a drop—I mean a *drop*—or you will be soooo sick." He procured a clean, dry glass from the far cabinet and filled it with water from a plastic tank under the window. "Don't brush your teeth in it. Don't open your mouth in the shower."

I did as told. I knew the water was *bad*. But I thought that was an American way of thinking about it. Obviously, Bolivians didn't get sick from the water in Bolivia.

Or so I assumed. But good, clean water was scarce—fewer than 50 percent of Cochabamba's inhabitants had access to piped water—and those without access were forced to buy water from a private company at exorbitant prices. Outraged citizens organized a demonstration in the city of Cochabamba and asked all businesses to shut their doors and for the people to march in the streets. This was the beginning of the Cochabamba Water Wars. Movies would be made about it, the way the public rose up to protest having something as basic as water denied them.

And I, ignorant, wide eyed, dizzy from elevation and the need for calories and my drug of choice, had wandered into the thick of the Cochabamba Water Wars.

I stumbled into an open pizzeria with bright orange decor and was told they did not serve coffee. I settled for tea and a slice of cheese pizza, and was staring sadly at the flaccid tea bag floating in a cup of lukewarm water when protesters flooded the streets of Cochabamba.

At first it was an exciting sound, the din of something happening after my sad, quiet morning in this gray, shuttered city. I left my table—I was the only one in the place, no need to worry about my backpack on the back of the chair—and stood with my teacup in the doorway.

From wall to wall, filling the street and the sidewalks, indigenous protesters flowed down the slope with the grace and speed of water. The women wore long braids and bowler hats, some with wide brims, and jaunty pleated skirts. They were a short and skin-weathered crowd. I took one woman to be around forty, but then saw the baby tied to her back with a blanket, observed her face more carefully, and realized she was probably in her twenties. Some wore pilly cardigan sweaters; no one carried placards to announce their position. One thing was noticeable: after a morning of being completely ignored, people were starting to turn their gaze toward me.

Just when I started to feel as if I was connecting with strangers—wasn't I being supportive of whatever was going on, standing here and smiling?—I felt a mean stinging blast against the skin of my legs. I was too confused to move. Then I saw three *cholitas* walking arm-against-arm, legs marching in unison, reach into satchels they had tied around their waists. Their fists emerged full of gravel and split-open fruit. Then they aimed the contents of their fists at me.

The proprietor dashed to pull down the metal grate of the pizzeria as I stood there, still unmoving, being pelted with wet mango and sharp tiny rocks.

"But what did I *do*?" I shouted at the *cholitas*. They smiled, and one threw back her head and laughed a satisfying-looking belly laugh. I was laughing too, despite the stinging down my legs, and we all kept laughing as she reached in for another dose of gravel and threw it at me. I ducked. The grate crashed down.

Inside the now-dark pizzeria, I stood shell shocked with fruit pulp dangling from my hair.

"Why?" I asked the proprietor, who was now mopping furiously, head bowed in anger or embarrassment.

"They're just crazy," he said.

"Is it because I'm American?" I asked.

"No," he said. "It's because they're crazy."

I eventually learned that the pizzeria had remained open when all businesses were supposed to be closed in support of the protest, and I was targeted because I was supporting their business; I held their teacup in my hand. But I didn't know that then. What I knew was that I was the only American around, and I didn't see fruit pulp dripping out of anyone else's hair.

Maybe it was the feeling of not being able to fight against my Americanness and what I represented in Bolivia that sent me running into the arms of Coke.

Aaron and I took a walk after school. The morning's aimless wandering had led me into a dead zone, and Aaron led me to the more appealing neighborhood, with a mind-blowing outdoor market and charming parks and plazas. At the market, *cholitas* sat in front of piles of chilies, potatoes, melons, and mystery fruits. Each item spilled out of its own woven plastic satchel, and everything was flawless and perfect. I carried a Nikon point-and-shoot film camera in my bag, and I snapped the requisite photographs of the market color, but what I really wanted to take pictures of were people, and Aaron had cautioned me against it, explaining that it often wasn't well received.

But when we came upon a plaza where a knot of *cholitas* sat silently in front of plastic satchels spilling coca leaves onto the pavers, I raised my camera.

"They're not going to like that," Aaron said. Indeed, as soon as they were aware of the angle of my lens, the women turned their heads away from me, and I was left with the blur of their braids and the backs of their heads. I may not have captured their faces, but I captured the slogans they'd scrawled onto cardboard with black marker: *coca sí, Yanquis no*, and, my favorite, *Yanqui go home*.

We sat at a café where there was no coffee.

"This is ridiculous," I said. "Doesn't anyone drink coffee in this city?"

I ordered water and Aaron ordered a Coke. "If you need a caffeine fix, why don't you have a Coke? Coke is everywhere."

"I didn't come to Bolivia to drink Coca-Cola," I said.

"Try coca tea, then," he suggested, and I did, but that drug was not *my* drug.

When Friday came, we flew to Sucre. We wandered the City of Four Names. Sucre had recently been named a World Heritage Site by UNESCO and had a colonial charm, including a massive cathedral and a general feeling of colorful history. Bleacher seats had been lined up in the main plaza, and we sat on them on Friday night and watched a music performance by men wearing ponchos of maroon, pink, and green stripes, blowing into pan flutes and keeping time with sheep-hoof shakers and small guitar-like lutes called *charangos*. We drank the local beer.

The next day we walked until we were too wilted from the heat to walk any further. Then we sat down at a table under a striped umbrella at a café. When Aaron's Coca-Cola came, he poured it into a droplet-free glass. There was something familiar about that sudden frost that appeared on the glass . . . something that gave me a really good feeling. A feeling from a long, long time ago . . . years ago; I had a flashback to my grandmother's musky pantry in Red Springs, North Carolina . . . there was something about that hobble-skirt bottle, the vessel that had been unappealingly plasticized in the United States, and the whisper of the fizz . . .

Aaron took a swallow and relaxed into his chair.

"Coca-Cola, *por favor*," I said to the waiter.

The bottle was cold as if it had been in an icebox. I waited for the fizz-foam to die and tilted the glass to my lips, swallowed. It was like my mouth had been stung by a family of benevolent arctic jellyfish babies.

Oh wow. Coke *was* it.

And then, the bottle was empty. Two hundred fifty milliliters was not very much Coke.

"I want another one," I told Aaron. He was three sips in.

Coke #2 was delivered promptly, and I tried a sip right from the bottle. Bubbles burst along the sides of my tongue. I felt fabulous. I was refreshed.

"Coke is it!" I exclaimed.

Aaron looked at me as if my head had spun around a few times. "What's wrong with you? Do you hear yourself?"

"I can't help it. I really love this Coke." I looked at the second empty bottle and gave it a pout.

Aaron exaggeratedly scooted his glass a little closer to him. "You might want to take it easy on the Coke," he said.

"Hey, you started me on this stuff," I said. "You drink it all the time. You told me I should get off coffee by getting on Coke!"

"Some of us can handle it," Aaron said.

Coca-Cola. The inviting white wave. Hoary sweat on the can. The feel of the solid bottle in my fist. The hiss as it hit the ice.

I was in bed with a bad dude.

First of all, Coke was packed with sugar and chemicals and was highly corrosive. It was impressively effective in removing rust from metal. I knew people to use it as a kind of chemical drain opener in Costa Rica, where Coca-Cola bottle caps were also used as vegetable graters. Coke's active ingredient was phosphoric acid. Couldn't be good for your digestive system, really, but handy when you needed to shine up your fender or polish your silverware.

I knew that Coke was terrible for you. Who didn't? Caffeine was hard on the body. The sodium benzoate in Diet Coke was even linked to DNA damage. Scientific evidence brought up in lawsuits showed that phosphoric acid caused no *immediate* harm. The question was—and always will be—when do you care more about how you feel later than how you might feel now?

And the cocaine thing—everyone knew that was true. Coca-Cola did once contain cocaine. Not just coca extract, a trace of which is still used in the Coca-Cola recipe. Nine millimeters per glass of *cocaine*. Doctors recommended it. Housewives revered it. I bet it went fabulously with cigarettes and sex.

Coca was the nice guy who threw the party, and Coke came and crashed it with all his flashy friends and trashed the house. Coke was the bully who stole coca's lunch money. And I was officially part of his clique.

To compound my foreigner status, Aaron took me to a restaurant he called the Rodizio, an Atkins diet paradise where enormous cuts of meat were carried out on dowel-like skewers by men with strong arms and sword-like carving tools. We watched an American business-man pay his bill, reaching into his wallet and pulling out a fistful of hundred-dollar bills, flashily riffling through them for the right num-ber to cover the large party he was entertaining.

"Gross," we said, and took another bite of lamb.

That was the night I woke up in a state of alarm, with shooting pains in my gut, and the sense that I should take measures to escape my own body.

I spent my night on the floor of the hall bathroom, groaning loudly, prone on the tile. There was no diarrhea and no vomiting, not yet. I spent almost all the dark hours of that night begging the gods to initiate either one of those things, but there was no relief, and I moaned on the tile until morning.

Aaron opened the bathroom door, already dressed for school. "Poor gringa," he said. "How long have you been lying here?"

"Hours," I groaned.

"What does it feel like?"

"Like someone is sharpening knives in my stomach."

"Did you drink the water?"

"Not intentionally."

"Maybe you opened your mouth in the shower," Aaron suggested. But I hadn't. I'd been careful, even though I'd thought at first, *but really, how sick could I get?*

Aaron brought me water and a hot mug of manzanilla. He placed it on the tile floor and rubbed my back. "I'm sorry I can't miss a day of school," he said. "What are you going to do about your trip to the Chapare?"

I was going to be sick wherever I was, I reasoned, so when I could peel myself off the floor, I was going to go catch a bus to the Chapare jungle.

I had already bought my ticket for the *trufi* and booked a night in the town of Villa Tunari. It was a seven-hour ride to the Chapare province. Chapare was where much of the illegal coca was grown, and though my excitement had been doused by discomfort, I still craved the traveler's delight of a long public bus ride, and it was only for one night. When I was no longer moaning out loud I packed my daypack, stumbled to the *trufi* depot, flopped into my assigned seat, and tried not to gag when the man next to me pulled a sulfur-smelling boiled egg from a plastic bag and ate it with his fingers.

Sacks were alive with chickens. Passengers dangled money out the windows, summoning girls and women shoving snacks. Our vehicle was an old American-style school bus with an electric blue exterior lumpy from multiple layers of paint. We chugged out of the station. The city scenery fell away and was replaced by an endless expanse, dips and mountains and fields, patches of color, mostly an intense, alive green. Indigenous families collected on blankets on fields of grass, the women in their bowler hats and jaunty skirts. If I didn't move the pain wasn't so bad. So I didn't consider moving, until a few hours in when the bus stopped at a little shack marked Control Coca and military officers ordered us off the bus.

"Yellow fever inoculations!" a soldier announced from the front of the bus. A sign outside my window warned of the high risk of yellow fever in the Chapare province, and announced the fact that everyone on the bus was required to get the shot unless they had proof of inoculation. The official wore a beret I couldn't help associating with Che Guevara. It gave me a radical thrill. His machine gun fell from a strap on his shoulder. I watched out the window as an old man was helped up to the flatbed of a truck, where he rolled up his sleeve and received a needle in the deltoid.

I was glad I'd gotten my yellow fever shot.

I remained in my seat. I hoped my gringa charm, which I tried not to use unless necessary, would work on the official coming down the aisle toward me.

"I'm pretty sick," I said in Spanish.

"Let's see your bag."

He dug around inside my daypack, feeling through my rolled-up clothes. He found no contraband. I unfolded the inoculations card I kept tucked into my passport. "Yellow fever," I said, and pointed.

"What kind of sickness do you have now?" he asked.

I put my hand on my stomach and gave the look of someone about to keel over.

"You should drink some coca tea," he said. He handed back my card and left.

At the "rustic hotel" in Villa Tunari, I was the only guest. I slid on my bathing suit and hiked a short way down to the Tunari River and waded in the gentle current. Because there was no one there to take pictures with, I held the camera at arm's length and took pictures of myself with the scenery behind me. The photos, when developed, showed me to be extremely pale.

Whatever had taken its stranglehold on my gut eased its grip. Butcher knives were now butter knives. I activated the outdoor water heater by turning the knob of the gas tank and inching the match toward the underside of the tank until the flame caught. I shooed what appeared to be flying cockroaches out of my room and took a shower once the water had time to heat. I crossed the grass to the main house to inform the proprietor I wouldn't be eating dinner.

"No dinner? Why?"

I was happy to have someone to talk to. "*Hombre*, did I get sick last night." I told him about the shooting pains and the sweaty forehead. I explained how carefully I'd avoided nonbottled water. I told him about the restaurant where Aaron and I had dined the night before: Rodizio, the weird and fancy foreigner place. "I think the restaurant was what made me sick," I said.

The proprietor's name was Arturo. He was tall and had thick black hair and a moustache. We sat on the patio of the main building, a large, round room with no walls covered with a thatched roof. The fact that it was empty except for us made me feel like Arturo and I were good friends who had found a nice place to perch together and talk. "I will bring you something to make you feel better," he said.

"Oh, I know what will make me feel better," I said. "When my stomach is upset I drink Coca-Cola." Arturo shook his head and disappeared into the kitchen, and returned with a steaming cup of pale green tea.

I hadn't gotten down more than a few sips of water since I'd gotten sick. I swallowed, waited. Everything seemed to be going well.

"Drink the whole cup," Arturo said, "if you can."

It was going down softly. Coca tea tasted grassy, like the yerba maté I had shared with Aaron, but sweeter. Its mellow flavor was in harmony with its light green hue. I liked the earthy aftertaste. It didn't magically cure me, but shortly after I was able to eat a small amount of rice.

"There you go," Arturo said with a smile.

He gave me two bags to take on the road. They were regular old tea bags, folded into paper like Lipton's. I tucked them into my journal.

Back on the bus, I watched the rolling hills out the window and wondered where all that coca was hidden. It would have been nice to at least catch a glimpse of the plant that caused so much trouble. The nice Bolivian girl sitting next to me offered me a cough drop. I felt I couldn't say no, so I thanked her and unwrapped it and placed it on my tongue. My stomach cramped with the first suck. The fight between my body and me wasn't over yet.

The bus broke down and stopped for an hour while three passengers climbed under the bus to help the driver diagnose the problem. No one seemed to be upset or in a hurry. Eventually, the driver started the engine and one man lifted a panel on the floor at the front of the bus and reached into the engine compartment. I watched his elbow pump as he pulled some engine part over and over by hand as the driver drove. He must have been in really good shape to keep it up like that. After fifteen minutes back on the road, another man took over. Bearing witness to this kind of public problem-solving, of volunteers stepping up for the benefit of the common good—instead of grumbling about the bus company or worrying about late arrivals—was one of the things I loved most about leaving the States. We passengers might have been strangers to each other, but for the length of this journey, we were in it together.

When we stopped again I thought the engine had died a second time. Through the window I saw the shack where we had stopped before, the little wooden house marked with the crude official sign. We were back at Coca Control. But this time, something exciting was happening. I leaned into the aisle to see through the windshield. The little *trufi* in front of us was being literally torn apart.

Stuffing flew out the door as a team of four officials cut open the seats and ripped the panels from the ceiling. They worked methodically. The *trufi* passengers, all of them older indigenous men and women, stood off to the side, watching.

I could read no expression in their black eyes or on their deeply wrinkled faces. No one looked frightened; no one wrung his or her hands. Past the checkpoint, *cholitas* stood at food stalls, but most of them had wandered into the road by now to witness the seizure.

We filed off the bus to observe. I stood on the side of the road with the nice girl who had given me the cough drop.

"Is this common?" I asked her.

"Not at all," she said. Her hand was over her mouth. Indeed, most of our bus gang wore expressions of concern and surprise. Where the road fell off, deep valleys and expanses of green spread out for miles. It was a spectacular, dramatic setting. I reached into my daypack for my camera.

I took a picture of a small old man in a straw hat getting cuffed. I took three pictures of the soldiers loading him onto the back of a covered truck. I took two pictures of a *cholita* running after the truck as it pulled away. Her braids swung behind her. I stood near the food stalls on the side of the road while I did this; that was the best vantage point, and while the *cholitas* from the stands didn't move away from me, they didn't reveal their feelings about what I was doing, either.

I lowered my camera when I saw the soldier walking in my direction, his gun steadied by a hand on the strap.

He was coming to confiscate my camera and film.

"*Hola*," I said, smiling my friendliest smile.

"Can you take a picture of me?" he asked. I looked at him blankly. He was probably eighteen or nineteen years old. He showed me his teeth through a sweet, shy smile. "Maybe a picture of me with one of my friends?" He pointed to the group of soldiers collected near the coca control shack. Two were trying to give the impression that they were not looking at us. I felt like I was being asked to dance.

"Yes," I said, "why not?" I thought I should explain. "But I can't show you the picture now. I have to go back to the United States and get the film developed first. You could give me your address and I could send you the photo. It might take a couple of weeks, though."

He waved his hand. "Ah, no. Too much trouble. Thank you!" His gun swayed as he made his way back to his friends.

"I've never gotten to see anything like that before," Aaron said when I told him about my bus ride.

I felt lucky that something exciting had happened during my trip to Bolivia, something distinctly Bolivian. It was a story with a climax, and I had great pictures to go along with it. Even the daily stomach cramping—which stayed with me for over a month whether I ate plain toast, pizza, white rice, or fried chicken—was like a souvenir. I returned home with a box of coca tea, and I drank it to ease my stomach pain. The effect was mild; it might have been a placebo. I drank it feeling as if I had been initiated into something.

But when I watched the truck drive away in the moment between the pictures I took and the conversation with the government official, I was on the outside, looking in from an untouchable position of safety.

After the official walked away, and before we reboarded the bus, I scanned the great bowl of the Chapare jungle from the checkpoint site, and a hand-painted sign caught my eye. It was about a foot tall, nailed at eye level to a tree. The outline of a hobble-skirt bottle was peeling away, but it was distinctive. *Siempre Coca-Cola*, the sign announced. The paint was faded and the wood was weathered, but the message, in the middle of nowhere, endured. I thought, yes, there will always be that, and there will always be consumers like me, so easy to seduce.

A few years later, in 2006, socialist activist Evo Morales was elected president of Bolivia. He was Bolivia's first indigenous president, a grower of coca, a former llama herder, and leader of the Cocalero union of coca farmers. When he took office—his literal office—he plastered the walls with the sweet leaves of the Andes. He'd always given the finger to the DEA and their war on drugs; now it was Bolivia's official policy, along with Evo's earnest goal that the citizens of his nation "live well." The cultivation of coca would live on, unimpeded.

It was a triumph for humanity, in my mind. The underdog had prevailed, righteousness had prevailed. I celebrated this, knowing, still, that in Bolivia, as in other countries I might visit, I was little more than an ambassador for the Bad Guys. Being armed with little knowledge but loads of goodwill had done nothing to change that fact, and the only thing I could do was own it, order another Coke.

But say I'd been a different kind of American. Not an American with a proud addiction, a cerebral American torn between a life of prestigious office jobs and the life of a vagabond who wanders into foreign lands with her eyes wide open and her head cleared out for all the things she wants to learn. Say, instead, I was an American who took her goodwill and lived according to it, actively. Who drove a biodiesel-fueled station wagon stickered with slogans about peace and tolerance, and came to Bolivia not just to absorb the culture but to actively fight against the injustices in the distribution of water and the coca control.

If I were that kind of American, I would have been in Cochabamba *because of* the Water Wars. Maybe I would have marched in the streets with the *cholitas* instead of watching them from the sidelines.

Then again, even if I were that kind of American, I would still be from a place where you can leave a faucet running while you clean your sink full of dishes. I would still live in a place where you could turn up your nose at a public drinking fountain because the filtered and treated water might be tainted from so many mouths that close to the spigot. The *cholitas* still might not want me. Maybe, if I were that better kind of American, they would still throw gravel at my pink skin. But maybe instead of running to hide from it, wrapping up my hurt in a Coca-Cola blanket, I would take off the shirt I wore for modesty, hike up my skirt, and offer more skin, saying, "Go ahead. I can take it."

THE BLIND MASSEUR
(Costa Rica)

I asked directions from a blind man. This was in the Marriott hotel just outside of San José, Costa Rica. The Marriott was a luxury hotel with a driving range, two pools, and complimentary brunch. It was staffed by men who insisted on carrying one's dirt-encrusted backpack even when one had a running rule to carry it oneself. Most important at present: there was a spa. For the past four weeks I had been sleeping on the floor of an unoccupied house in the sleepy town of El Silencio. I was there to lead a volunteer team of sixteen Americans. The floor of the unoccupied house where I slept with the other female volunteers was poured cement and my body had been cushioned only by an inch-thick inflatable mattress. I was just about ready for a massage.

The path to the spa was a maze of tiled hallways and colonial arches and courtyards with fountains. I wandered in circles, lost. A man, whose back was to me, was holding the receiver of a pay phone, about to hang it up. He wore a work uniform, overalls. I called out to him, "*Perdón?*"

The man turned. I saw the milky eyes, and then the walking stick came tapping in an arc toward me. I saw that he was blind. He looked to be about thirty years old, but his hair was older than he was, though there was still more pepper in it than salt. He had that dreamy, faraway look that has made me feel envy toward blind people. Even while the blind man was here, he appeared to be somewhere better. I said, "Oh, no. I'm sorry. I was just looking for the spa." He pointed toward the hallway I'd already been down. "Thank you," I said, because I didn't want to embarrass myself or the blind man by admitting I was still confused.

Eventually, after further wandering, I found the door from under which seeped the scent of lavender. I booked a massage for later in the afternoon.

Upstairs, I flopped on the bed in gratitude for sheet-bleach and the *Miami Herald* I'd jacked from the lobby, of which I would read every word. During my four weeks in El Silencio I had read nothing but Dostoyevsky's *Crime and Punishment*, which disturbed me more deeply than I'd anticipated. It was the only reading material I had brought with me. I had not realized that the majority of the novel was about the character's moral anguish and that the "punishment" was largely something that happened inside his head. I was hungry for less claustrophobic stories, and for news, among other things.

I didn't require a hotel room such as this. I'd slept in my share of six-dollar hotel rooms I did not much like, and some six-dollar hotels I found perfectly comfortable. A twenty-dollar hotel was a safe bet for me. But I'd heard talk of this new hotel, the Marriott on the old coffee plantation; I'd heard from a gringa friend that she took the bus from San José just for the Sunday brunch buffet. The Marriott gleamed and pampered. It would make me forget the coldness of the concrete floor and the taste of rice and beans, if only for one day. The bedding here was not worn or stiff from too much laundering. The faucets were free of rust blisters. The french doors had fresh paint; they opened onto the close-mowed driving range. Coffee had once grown where there was now a fairway.

Aside from my friend Andrés—a friend from my old life in Costa Rica, the town where I'd spent the year—I was keeping the fact that I was staying in the Marriott a secret.

On this, my most recent stay in Costa Rica, I'd helped build a new school with seventeen other Americans and a rotating crew of El Silencio residents. We stacked cement blocks, twisted metal wires around rebar, and constantly mixed cement and carted it around, with great effort, in wheelbarrows. The El Silencians were gracious, and grateful for our desire to haul *bloc* with them, if not confused. Why were we building schools here, instead of in our own towns, back home in America?

This had never occurred to us as an option. We were all from towns that contained multiple schools built by professional construction teams who would not have wanted our help had we offered it.

I hadn't told my new friends in El Silencio that I was spending the night in the Marriott because as far as they knew, the Marriott was not for people like me. I was like them: I ate everything with a big spoon, cleaned dirt from my fingernails every afternoon, and showered according to when the water in the pipes would be warmed by the sun. The Marriott was for those elusive gringos who come here for guided tours to the beach or butterfly farm. Those gringos did not speak Spanish, and they had no taste for plantains the way plantains were fried in Costa Rica. The prices inside the hotel compound were American prices: A bucket of golf balls cost ten dollars, a bucket that empties fast. Not to mention how dear a cheese pizza was—and I was getting the cheese pizza, along with a nice glass of wine. I'd been living on rice and beans and fried bread for a month.

Dave, my former director, had married a sharp, warm, and stylish *tica* named Karina and they now lived in San José. They were expecting me the following day, and I did not tell them I was staying here either. I preferred to keep my indulgences between the bellhops and myself. I ordered room service and watched HBO *Olé!* for an hour. Then I went back to the salon for my massage.

The man at the desk introduced me to my massage therapist, who turned out to be the blind man.

I was aware that there was such a phenomenon as the blind masseur and his female counterpart, the blind masseuse. Historically, the blind were valued for the sharpness of their other senses. Now, especially in Asia, the blind were schooled in massage therapy because it was one of the only careers available to the blind. In South Korea, only the blind were legally allowed to practice medical massage. In Cambodia, those whose eyes had been assaulted by the Khmer Rouge—those who, for instance, had battery acid thrown in their faces—were sought out by societies for the blind. Training them as massage therapists elevated them from their only alternative, which was poverty. It was community service. But there was no such society of blind masseurs in Costa Rica, and poverty here was not so extreme.

"Hello," I said to the blind man, keeping the surprise out of my voice. I'd thought he was some kind of janitor, because of his overalls. "I think I asked directions from you earlier."

"You were looking for the spa," the blind man said. "Well, you found it!" He led me to a room down a short hall. The room was dimly lit, almost too dark. I wondered if the blind man knew this. He instructed me to undress, but he did not add that option usually offered in American salons: to your level of comfort.

What was my level of comfort? It wouldn't matter if the blind man stayed in the room or left the room, in terms of what the blind man might see of me that I didn't want him to see. Then I realized that the sound of my undressing might embarrass me for him to hear. I'm not one of those people who believes that blind people physically hear better than people who can see. I believe they might listen harder. To me, the act of undressing was more exposing than the fact of being naked underneath a sheet. But the masseur left before I had to face any feelings of awkwardness.

I was on my back, naked under a sheet, when the blind man returned. He told me his name was Juan Carlos. "I'm so glad you speak Spanish," he said. "Most gringos who come here don't speak Spanish."

This wasn't the first time a massage therapist had kept me from falling off the cliff of consciousness. My idea of a good massage involved dulling down my brain, stamping out thought. I wanted nothing to do with language, and he expected me to talk. Did I like Costa Rica? Indeed, I liked it very much, even felt at home here. How did I know Spanish? I'd lived here before. Where had I lived? The town was a small town near Juan Viñas, so small it wasn't on a map and he wouldn't have known of it.

"I may know of it." With his posture and a curl of the lips, Juan Carlos was showing signs of a cockiness that was familiar to me in Costa Rican men. But how had he learned the cocky lip curl? "This is my country," he said. "What's the name of the town?" I told him the name of the town. He'd never heard of it.

"Told you," I said.

Then I asked him some questions. How long had he been blind? He was born blind. How did he get trained as a massage therapist? Oh, he'd learned from different people. Where did he live? In San José, the city. How did he get home from the hotel? He took the bus, of course, like everybody else.

Right around my left knee Juan Carlos said, "You have nice legs."

Andrés, when I lived in his small sugar-cane town, told me more than once that I had nice legs.

"And I can see that *you* like your legs," Andrés said, pointing down to where my palms were placed flat on the tops of my thighs. In our town, where I taught children, where I had to be an example, and where a good number of the parents had recently discovered Jesus and the fact that there were a lot of things Jesus didn't want you to do, I had to dress conservatively. When I was away from the town, I preferred a particular plaid miniskirt. It was extremely short. When I sat on the stool across from Andrés in the cantina in Juan Viñas, I kept my hands on my legs, delighted by their bareness.

One time Andrés took me around back outside his friend Gallo's house, used his hands to press my back to the wall, and smiled. We had known each other eight or nine months and had not yet kissed. Of course, this was my decision. Andrés had always come on hard. There were a few reasons we had never so much as kissed before. One was that I was not going to confirm the stereotype of the Easy Gringa. Also, if it got back to anyone in our town—which meant everyone in our town—I would suddenly be defined as that, the girl who'd hooked up with Andrés. He was smart, one of the few from town that would go to Universidad, but the people in the town had a certain idea of him: he was poor, and he was cocky. They would make me pay if I rewarded him with my sexual attention.

But especially, I knew that should I lose my mystery, Andrés would value me not more, but less. That's how it worked with mystery.

So far, he was my best friend, and I didn't want to give that up.

Andrés ran his hands down the sides of my bare thighs and said, "Nice." That night I was wearing a short gray baby doll dress. I'd been drinking more beer than usual of late, because I'd started hanging out more with Andrés, and we usually hung out in bars. Andrés ran his hand up my dress and rested it on my stomach.

"You haven't been going to the gym, lately, have you?" he joked, and squeezed at my belly fat.

Andrés didn't get past second base that night, or anytime after that, either. That's what he got for bad manners.

All of this was a long time before the night I spent in the Marriott.

Juan Carlos had a good attitude about being blind.

"I have a good job. I have a good family. What I don't have is a girlfriend," he said, in that ambiguous way that might mean he was hitting on me, or might not.

"Does your blindness make you a better massage therapist?"

"I think so," Juan Carlos said. "I don't think I would be a better massage therapist if I were not blind. The bottom line is, I make people feel good. I feel I'm doing them a service. Maybe it helps that I can't see my clients—it helps them relax."

Juan Carlos said he had a good family. He would not go hungry without this job. It was different elsewhere. In 2008, in South Korea, the government threatened to open the business to the sighted. The blind masseurs panicked. Twenty-six of them stood on a bridge and threatened to jump. Two did jump. A few others set fire to a car.

The stakes elsewhere were higher.

"I do it for fun," Juan Carlos said.

Juan Carlos had worked his way down my IT band and aching calf. Now his hands were on my right foot, his thumbs pushing into my instep. It hurt in a good way.

"Nice feet, too," he said.

"You know, I've had my share of massages," I said, "and I've never had a massage therapist give me so much feedback on what parts of my body were 'nice.'"

A short while later his hands found my stomach. "Uh oh," he said. "Not so good."

I laughed out loud: he had to be kidding me. I had to give another lecture to another *machista*. "Look, Juan Carlos, permit me to say something. My belly might not *look* good, if you're going by conventional standards, if you're looking at skinny models in magazines, which obviously you're not because you're blind, but I happen to think it *feels* good." He was smiling above me, looking proud of himself for some reason. I took a liberty. "You," I said, "of all people, should appreciate my *panza*."

Juan Carlos said, "I just think you should work out a little."

Once Andrés looked me in the eye and told me quite seriously that he would live with me if I wanted, and then began talking about neighborhoods he liked in San José. The way he spoke of this was not romantic. Nor did it seem calculating; it did not seem to be about gringa money, entirely—he simply seemed determined to get somewhere, and he wanted me to come with him. He didn't belong in that tiny sugar cane town, and neither did I. He seemed to think that we could escape together and have a good life being who we really were.

Andrés's friend Gallo had just moved in with a gringa, and she would probably never go back to the States. There were expats like that in Costa Rica, tons of them—the ones who could never go home again, for whom Costa Rica was not just an exotic time-out from regular life. There were plenty of things to keep you anchored in the

United States: Pizza Hut, the mall in San Pedro, the Marriott Hotel. And of course there were reasons Costa Rica might be a better place to live: low taxes for Americans, a perfect climate, beaches and wildlife beyond compare.

I was not one of those expats. Andrés thought I might be, because as many times as I'd left Costa Rica, I always came back. I'd been back within a year of leaving to see everyone I missed, and I went back to attend Dave and Karina's wedding, and I'd been back on behalf of Putney Student Travel to set up a new program in the sleepy town of El Silencio. Then I'd been back to lead the trip.

Yes, there was something about the place that made me return again and again. But still, home was always in the back of my mind. Home was not here, though I felt *at* home here.

I didn't want Costa Rica to lose its mystery. I didn't want it to be home. I wanted it to be different from home, and I wanted its difference to embrace me. As with my extended flirtation with Andrés, I liked the combination of comfort and potential and mystery.

How much mystery must you face, being blind?

At the end of my massage, Juan Carlos asked me the color of my eyes. I told him my eyes were brown.

"Ooh. That's too bad. It would be much better if they were blue."

"Didn't you tell me you've been blind all your life?"

"Since I was born. What about your hair?"

"*Macha macha*"—the standard line. Not just light brown, but real blond.

"Oh, that's good, good!"

"You don't even know what color *is*!" I said.

"I just know blue eyes are better," Juan Carlos said. "Blond hair. I just know."

There were some things you just knew. You knew, if you were Costa Rican, that blond hair was scarce, and therefore valued. You knew the same thing about blue eyes. You didn't need to see these things with your eyes in order to believe them.

"Do you want to go out somewhere tonight?" Juan Carlos asked. "Somewhere in San José?"

"Does it have french windows and room service and HBO *Olé!*?"

Juan Carlos laughed. "No."

"Then, thank you, but I think I'll stay here."

I wouldn't have gone out with Juan Carlos anyway, but the truth was, I was expecting Andrés later that evening.

Before I left El Silencio, I made a furtive trip to the public phone at the *pulpería* and called Andrés to tell him about my reservation at the Marriott. He agreed to visit me. I even cleared it with reception at the hotel; sometimes Costa Ricans weren't allowed in gringo rooms unless their names were on the register. It felt like a big decision. I was going to let Andrés see, for the first time, that I had the kind of money that enabled me to sleep at a place like the Marriott. We would be sealed into a room with a door that shut tightly and closed out sound, something that did not exist in the town where he lived. We would be alone, really alone, for the first time, and there would be no nearby witnesses to instruct us on how to judge our actions. It was part of the hotel employees' job to keep their opinions to themselves.

I stopped at the bar on the way back to my room and ordered a glass of white wine. I took it with me, sipping on the way. I put on loose pants that had been washed in the pila and line dried. I put on my favorite black shirt, and I didn't care that the clothes would get greasy with massage lotions, because I liked the smell and feel of the oils on my skin. I left a trail of lavender fumes behind me in the corridor.

I waited.

I listened for a knock on the door. I flipped through the channels, lingered on the German station, visited CNN for a while, then went back to the bar for another glass of wine.

Around ten, I put the chain on and ran a bath.

In the morning, I repacked my backpack, folding my clothes neatly and feeling disappointed.

Before I left I took a piece of hotel stationery out of the desk and wrote Andrés a letter. I told him, in a complicated fashion, that it was too bad he didn't come to see me because who knew when I would be back again. I wrote my return address in the upper left corner. I licked and adhered a Costa Rica blue morpho butterfly postage stamp that I still had tucked into my wallet from the last time I'd been in Costa Rica and slipped it into the box, a fancy container made of carved and polished rainforest wood, in the hotel lobby.

One month later, the same letter arrived in my mailbox in Vermont. I was shocked to find it in the slot. It was sealed as if it had never been opened. Had Andrés forwarded it to my home in the United States, needing me to see he hadn't read it? That didn't seem like him.

The envelope was rubber-stamped Insufficient Postage—Return to Sender. A fifteen-cent stamp would not get my letter from San José to his town two hours away, so they sent it to the United States for a quarter of the required postage. I opened the letter and read it, as if it had been intended for me.

Of the two of us, me and Andrés, I was the one who would understand it.

This is a truth about leaving the culture that raised you and crossing into another: We leave home with an arsenal of things we know about the place we're going. There is no disarming all of what we know, no matter how much touching and kneading and feeling we do, no matter how much we think we're trying. What makes us blind is what we *think* we see.

All Americans are rich. Blond hair and blue eyes are better. All Asians are *chinos*. Nicaraguans are criminals. Disney World is where true happiness resides.

A man wearing overalls with the hotel insignia is a janitor. A blind person doesn't know his way down the hall. Life is easier and simpler in Costa Rica, and Costa Ricans are such a happy people. But the men are all *machista*, and they all want the same thing. It doesn't matter if these things are true. I *know* them.

ONE SIDE OF THE STORY
(Nicaragua)

Diego and I hit it off at once. First of all, he could talk to me. I mean actually converse, which was unusual for him in his profession. Diego was my Spanish teacher, and I was the enigmatic student who came to the school in León who already spoke Spanish.

Within five minutes of our first meeting, Diego laid his pen on the table and closed the book he'd intended to use on my first day of instruction. "What are you doing at a Spanish school in Nicaragua?" he asked me. "You don't need Spanish classes."

"I have a job in Cuba that starts next month," I said. "My Spanish is rusty. And I never really did master the past subjunctive." In fact, there were several reasons I had come to spend a couple of spring weeks in Nicaragua, the past subjunctive and my upcoming teaching gig being only two of them. But I had Diego on "Cuba."

He picked up his book of poetry and rattled it. It was an anthology of Sandinista poetry, which, as I would soon learn, was Diego's passion. "You are so lucky!" Diego said. "It is a dream of mine to go to Cuba! Do you know the Cuban poet José Martí? Do you know that we are about to have another election here in Nicaragua and that the Sandinistas might win? *Viva la Revolución!*"

Diego agreed to spend most of the week drilling me in the past subjunctive, that pesky tense. For some backward reason, I could only grasp irregular verb forms in the past subjunctive. *I wish I had my camera. If only I could go back and do things differently.* But throw a regular verb at me and I wound up verbally butchering my hopes and doubts to the point of word salad.

But what Diego really wanted to teach me about was revolutionary poetry. He was a Sandinista, and obsessed, *obsessed* with Cuba. In love, really.

When I talk about love here I am not talking about romantic love. I mean magnetism. I mean the plain old feel-good love: you behold something, it makes you feel good. Things I was in love with in this way: coffee; my falling-apart Webster's dictionary; old episodes of *Beverly Hills, 90210*; hot, sweaty, spaghetti-strap days in New York City; a Costa Rican ice-cream snack called Trits; certain words, like *whiplash*; my indestructible Reef flip-flops with the ridges on the bottom; and, lately, Tylenol PM.

I fell in that kind of love with Diego the way you fall in love with a book based on its first chapter. I loved his enthusiasm about politics and poetry, and, frankly, I appreciated his interest in me. When I first get to a country—when I got to Costa Rica, for instance, and met the family who would host me for a year—I'm not surprised if my hosts are so excited to show me their lives and their country that they don't consider that I have a life somewhere else. This is fine with me; I know how to be patient, and I know that eventually we'll have mutual interest in each other's lives. But after my trip to Bolivia, where I couldn't shake the feeling of being ignored and then pelted with fruit and gravel, I didn't take personal connection abroad for granted. I was grateful for Diego and our instant, easy conversation.

The Spanish school centered on a small courtyard with a fountain. Off the courtyard were an office and two classrooms. Diego and I sat at a table at the back of the courtyard, drinking hot coffee in the warm April air and translating poetry for the day.

"Look at all this hope here!" Diego said, his finger pressing down on the page of text, a poem by Sandinista poet Ernesto Cardenal. "I have real hope that we can win this election." I was not used to hanging out with far-left-wing believers in Central America; La Victoria could not have been more apolitical. And it was different from hanging out in the library with the "socialists" at my liberal American college. It was different because here, in Nicaragua, radical left-wing governments actually took power. It was not just an idea. I projected a week-long honeymoon with socialist theory, coffee, and Diego. Little did I know that my first day with Diego would be my last.

There was a reason I'd chosen Nicaragua, in particular, as my destination.

According to the large majority of the people I'd talked to in Costa Rica, los Nicas were a despicable people. They were a violent society—just look at their history. Also, their Spanish was ugly. And so were their faces.

"They only come here to steal, rob, and kill people," my friend, a coffee farmer, said of Nicaraguan immigrants.

I asked another friend, a liberal law student: "Do you think Nicaraguans only come here to steal, rob, and kill people?"

"Yes," the law student said.

From time to time I visited my friend Andrés at his family's home at the other end of town. More than half the times I entered the house, I was greeted by the sight of his stepfather sunk into the couch, watching soccer on the television. He never looked up or offered me a greeting, which was an extreme oddity when presented with a guest. Andrés's sister and brother flocked to kiss me on the cheek, his mother rushed out a plate of hard toast and butter, and we all sat around the kitchen table and talked; no one addressed Andres's stepfather or acknowledged him at all. I found the whole situation bizarre. At the very end of the year, as Andrés and I walked away from his house to catch the bus, Andrés's eyes got wild and he said, "Alden, I have to tell you something."

"What?" I asked, alarmed.

"My stepfather . . . he's Nica." He stared at me, waiting for a reaction, and when I gave him none, he said it again: "He's Nica." He said it with amazement and shame, and suddenly it all became clear. This man was slumping back in his couch giving everyone the finger before they could give it to him, because he knew what it meant to be despised on principle.

I'm not saying all Costa Ricans felt this way. I certainly had friends there who worried about racism, classism, and xenophobia in a country that was beginning to seriously depend on Nicaraguans for their manual labor. But the sentiment was strong, and extended well beyond the borders of our cloistered town in the mountains.

I was pretty sure there was another side to the story.

The Spanish school placed me with a Nicaraguan family down the street from the school. This was another reason I'd hooked up with a school. Living with a family connected me to the community. And, instantly, I loved my host "mom," Doña Martha. She was a widow whose husband, a lawyer, had died sixteen months ago.

"I'm still very sad," Doña Martha told me as we drank coffee in her kitchen, and I put my hand over her hand when tears pooled in her eyes.

Also living in the house were Doña Martha's teenaged son, Danilo; a Japanese boarder named Yasito; a homeless alcoholic Doña Martha let sleep on the couch from time to time; and a toy dog who had just given birth to a litter and who'd peed with excitement the minute I stepped over the threshold. Her daughter, María del Pilar, and María del Pilar's boyfriend came and went.

It was lively at Doña Martha's house.

Doña Martha asked me why I spoke Spanish.

"I've spent a lot of time in Costa Rica," I said. "I lived there for a year."

"I lived in Costa Rica for ten years!" she said.

I was surprised and excited to hear this. "Did you like living there?" I asked.

"Not really," Doña Martha said. "They treat Nicaraguans like they have leprosy."

"*Sí*," I said, "in my experience, Costa Ricans aren't very hospitable to Nicaraguans."

"I don't understand who would want to live outside of his own country," Doña Martha said. "Who would ever do that willingly? It's very ugly." I had another opinion on this, but Doña Martha and I were coming from different places. I had only ever left my country out of choice.

"When the Sandinistas came," Doña Martha said, "we had no choice. We had to flee. We were afraid for our lives. Bombs fell, and we didn't know where they would land."

"My teacher at the school is a Sandinista," I said, expecting Doña Martha to give me a look of dismay, but she didn't. "He thinks they'll win again at this election."

"I'm afraid that might happen," Doña Martha said, nodding. "But I don't think they will."

I sipped at my coffee. Doña Martha wrung her hands.

It was April. The land around León was parched from a season of no rain. On my ninety-three-kilometer drive from Managua—the flattest city I'd ever seen, leveled by the earthquake of 1972 and never rebuilt—I'd marveled at the brownness of it all. The fields, the sun-darkened boys holding live iguanas up for drivers to buy, the straw hats they wore, the ponies pulling carts: all shades of brown and tan.

Dust and tumbleweeds blew through the narrow streets of León. The hills in the distance were leached of color, though they would soon become green, once the rains came. It was so hot that even street dogs knew to walk on the shady side of the street, holding tight to the walls, clinging to the shadows.

It was not the tourist high season. There was only one other student at the school, a surly and strikingly handsome nineteen-year-old German named Kristian who was traveling all over Latin America by himself. Nicaragua was his first stop. I'd seen him slink into the classroom with his meek-looking teacher, a small young woman in a too-loose knee-length skirt. Now we noticed each other in the court-yard, and he approached me without smiling.

"How is your teacher?" he asked me in English.

"Do you want to speak English or Spanish?" I asked, in the spirit of Spanish school.

"I don't speak Spanish. I don't speak any Spanish. That's why I'm *here*."

"Oh. Okay." I was disappointed that the one English speaker in my new little world seemed mean and scary. "My teacher's amazing. How is yours?"

"She's stupid and boring. I hate her."

Kristian marched into the administrative office. Within a few minutes, Flavia, the school director, pulled me aside and informed me that because Diego spoke fluent English, and the German demanded a teacher who spoke English, despite the school's stated and restated policy that all teaching was done entirely in Spanish, they were switching our teachers. I would now be working with Marla. As long as it was okay with me. What could I say?

"That German is not very nice," Flavia said, looking bullied.

Marla spent the day flipping through books, trying to figure out something to teach me.

"I want to work on the past subjunctive," I said.

Marla hummed. Her eyes scanned the wall behind me. I could see she wasn't sure what the past subjunctive was. I didn't want to tell her how to do her job, so I held myself back from suggesting she go home and read about it for tomorrow. She handed me a novel and I read aloud from it, stopping when I didn't know a word, and then she'd tell me what the word meant. It was a tedious lesson. I craved a cup of coffee, the universal cure for boredom.

"Do you want to call it a day and just go hang out and drink coffee?" I asked. Marla looked hugely relieved. We left the school together, and I looked over my shoulder for Diego, but he was off in the world with Kristian, the German thief.

I dragged a nagging sad feeling back to Doña Martha's house. Doña Martha was boiling penne pasta and grating a hard, yellow cheese. These were signs of wealth in Central America, as cereal is a sign of wealth. Her house was grander than any I'd stayed in in Costa Rica: past the foyer, the space opened to a ceiling-less garden, a jungle of tall green plants. When it rained, it rained within the walls of Doña Martha's house. Lizards scampered through the kitchen and zipped up the walls in the sitting room. My room was in the front of the house on the side of the noisy city street. Doña Martha, Danilo, and Yasito lived in the back.

"He pays the bills," Doña Martha said, pointing her cheese grater at Yasito, who sat at the other end of the table, eating. Yasito smiled with his teeth full of bread. You could see the love in this odd pair. "When my husband died I had to take people in to help pay for things."

The homeless man slept on the couch for free. His name was Miguelito. He couldn't have weighed a hundred pounds. His plaid shirt was dirt mottled, and he reeked of guaro. "I let him come and sleep on the couch whenever he wants," Doña Martha said. "He helps out with chores. I know what it's like to go through hard times. When the Sandinistas were in power, we had nothing. You couldn't even buy toothpaste. When we went to Costa Rica we didn't send money back to our relatives in Nicaragua. We sent food."

What interested me was that I'd always thought of the Costa Rican attitude toward Nicaragua as a class issue. The majority of Nicas who'd crossed the border into Costa Rica in recent history had done so because they were poor and had more opportunities in Costa Rica than they did in Nicaragua. But Doña Martha fled to Costa Rica for the opposite reason: She was one of the "haves," and she was fleeing the Sandinistas because of her *upper* class. Still, she was not exempt from contempt.

"If you ask me," Doña Martha said, "Costa Rica is a country with a superiority complex, and a country of tourism rather than history. Say what you want about the violence, violence is always ugly, but you can't say we don't have an interesting culture. And León survives!"

It was the slogan of the city—León survives. It was a good reminder that no matter what happened, whoever we were, we would carry on.

As Kristian had suggested, Marla was a sub-par instructor.

We started our second class by staring at each other across the desk.

"Uhh . . ." Marla said. "Mmmm . . ."

She gazed at the desktop looking nervous. I had uncharitable reactions to her insecurity, partially because I was paying for actual instruction and didn't think I should have to be responsible for carrying the conversation.

I gazed at Diego, across the courtyard drilling Kristian. The poetry books were pushed off to the side.

"So, what are we doing today?" I asked Marla.

Marla gave me some worksheets on the past subjunctive and told me to take them home. She'd correct them tomorrow.

"Right now we're going to the zoo."

Once Marla and I got out of our student-teacher roles and became a couple of girls walking down the street together, the situation improved. We talked about the restoration of the cathedral. It was buttercup yellow, and it dwarfed the visitors hanging about its steps. I asked her about the murals of Sandino and Che Guevara we passed on the streets. León was, historically, the left-wing city, and its public art advertised this. This was why I'd chosen it over its sister city, Granada, the historically conservative city, and the one more popular with foreigners.

"What do you think about the upcoming elections?" I asked Marla.

"Mmm," she said. "I don't know."

"What's the difference between the Sandinistas and conservatives here?" I asked.

"The Sandinistas have a black and red flag and the conservatives have a green flag."

I waited for Marla to crack a smile. I thought she might be quoting a line from a García Márquez novel or making a funny joke. She was not.

"What about what they believe in?" I asked.

"They're the same."

"Will you vote for the Sandinistas?" I asked this despite my suspicion that Marla wasn't planning to vote.

"I don't think so," she said. "Last time the Sandinistas were in power we couldn't get deodorant."

The Parque Zoológico Arlen Siú was in the barrio called Sutiava. Luckily, I'd worn sturdy shoes. Sutiava was a long hike away from the center of León, and was one of the poorer neighborhoods of the city, "pure indigenous," Marla said. It had been called Subtiava until 1995, at which point the city officially excised the *b*, thus removing the inferiority suggested by the prefix *sub*. The land and the people were darker here. The dry, caked dirt in the park near the church square was richer and redder. Children were everywhere, running happily wild. A wrinkled man with a red baseball cap hissed at Marla and me as we rounded a corner. "The only thing the men on the corners serve for," Marla said loudly, "is to annoy." I liked it when Marla got sassy. She was starting to feel like a friend.

At the entrance to the zoo was an unattended booth. We followed the concrete path to a series of cages. There was a *pizote*, which looked like a cross between an anteater and a raccoon, and squirrels, which were darker, thinner, and more agile than the species I knew from home, running around in square enclosures. Cages held rabbits, parrots, turkeys, and, bizarrely, chickens. A small boy poked a cheese puff through the bars of the monkey cage, where small white-faced monkeys sat still in the trees. Upon spotting the cheese puff, two monkeys hurled themselves at the bars. The boy's father grabbed his son and lifted him out of reach; the monkeys screeched, wrapping their paws around the bars like hardened criminal prisoners.

"They seem kind of . . . nasty," I said to Marla.

"I think they're hungry," she said.

"What a tragedy," the man with the small son said, while his son alternated between eating a cheese puff and throwing a cheese puff toward the cage. "This place seems abandoned. I don't think anyone's taking care of it at all."

Three alligators sat in inches of murky water in a concrete pool, unmoving. The jaws of one were open, its massive set of teeth hovering over nothing. Sickly green moss was growing inside its mouth, on its face.

On the walk home, as I fought sad thoughts of animals abandoned in cages, Marla took my arm and we strolled toward the center of the city like old friends. "I really didn't like that German," she confessed. "I hope I have something to teach you, but I'm glad I don't have to work with *him* anymore." I told her I didn't think he was very nice either, and also, he was very young, alone, and far from home, so he was probably having a difficult time.

"Why do people leave their lives behind like that, and when they're so young?" Marla asked. Marla had never left Nicaragua. It was too big a question to address. There were many reasons people left their lives behind.

"Do you have a boyfriend?" she asked.

"No," I said. It was always a popular question from the friends I made abroad, and for now I gave the easiest answer.

Here's the story I had come to Nicaragua to avoid.

Until recently, I did have a boyfriend. I met Jomar in Vermont, at an artists' colony, where he impressed me with his unstoppable drive to create. When he put his first marks on a canvas, he seemed to be going for something abstract: isolated gashes of color appeared at random upon the rectangular field. Then, all at once, whole images emerged: a fishbowl on a table, a girl reading a book. I loved watching him paint and the smell of his studio and his clothes. He was racially ambiguous and constantly fielded inquiries about his ethnic background; he was Chinese, Filipino, Polish, and Lithuanian, but strangers often approached him speaking Spanish. This, and his confident, positive nature and inclusive smile, gave him the quality of being able to fit in across all kinds of social boundaries. Everyone liked him, and he had a dimple so deep he could pop a grape into it when he smiled and it would stay.

We lived together in Vermont, each working part-time jobs, me in the Putney barn and he waiting tables, and spending the bulk of our days making art in our studio overlooking the Connecticut River. In addition to writing, I shot black-and-white film on the Nikon my father had bought in Japan before I was born, and spent one day a week making prints in the back darkroom of a photography gallery in Brattleboro. Our studio was hung with Jomar's drawings and my photographs, and the walls were lined with books. It was an idyllic life. But then three things happened.

One: I turned twenty-seven. Twenty-seven. I'd considered it an inconsequential year. But something about twenty-seven said that I was no longer young, and it was not enough to have done some cool traveling and held a series of jobs that didn't necessarily connect to each other. I was supposed to be building something. Could I call myself a writer? I did call myself that—I *wrote*—but I wasn't confident I'd earned the official title. I was writing consistently, and was pleased with some of the work I'd produced. I landed travel writing assignments from glossy magazines that paid well, and acceptance letters from literary magazines began to trickle in. But when I tried the longer form—I enrolled in the low-residency MFA program at Bennington, where I started and then abandoned a novel—I knew I was not ready to write a book; I was better at the short form, and better off, at least for now, perfecting the short form, and I was on a longer-than-expected road to my goal of authoring actual books.

Perhaps conversely, the more alarming thing about turning twenty-seven was that friends from high school, and even one or two friends from college, were starting to get married and buy homes in suburban towns and—ugh!—*have babies*. I was appalled by this. We were too young! Why were they throwing in the towel? How could they run into the arms of the familiar, and why so soon? I wanted nothing to do with this kind of behavior, and feared the consequences of settling down. Yet when you were in a stable relationship with someone wonderful, that was, ultimately, what you did. Was this—wiping spit-out Cheerios off some table in New Jersey—my fate?

What about my dreams of going to India? And Cambodia? You couldn't take *babies* places like that. Jomar and I would have made excellent babies, we thought, and the subject was broached. But when it was, it was quickly followed by nervous questions: What about our *work*? Our work came first. And what about staying open to the twists and turns of life and to adventures we couldn't have if we were tied down?

Two: Jomar applied, on a whim, to a Master of Fine Arts program in Boston, and was accepted. I had no interest in moving to Boston. But Jomar promised me it would be only a year, and then we would go back to New York, where we belonged. I bade farewell to our idyllic Vermont art-making life and began my job search. I secured a position teaching undergraduate creative writing at Emerson College, an arts and communication college in downtown Boston where the students were serious and fashionable and creative, and considered that a good consolation. I could do that for a year.

Three: It turned out that staying open to the twists and turns of life included being open to intimacies with other people. This was true first for Jomar, and then it was true for me.

After Jomar's small indiscretion, we stayed together, but a chip had been cut in my confidence. Combine that with a fear of entering the age of "growing up," and what does a confused late-twenty-something do?

Why not fall in love with someone terrified of attachment, socially incompatible with me, and very, very young? Maybe—I don't know—a *girl*? That would certainly slow my progress toward a conventional adulthood.

That was what I did.

The summer of my twenty-eighth year, I unpacked a suitcase in my dorm room at Amherst College, where I was teaching creative writing for the summer. I was three days behind everyone else on the staff. My ninety-four-year-old grandfather had passed away, and I'd missed

Orientation to attend his funeral services. I knew only a handful of the people I'd be working with.

A young resident adviser I'd met in passing appeared in my open doorway. I was folding shirts and placing them in rickety dresser drawers.

"I just threw up!" she exclaimed.

I was startled by her forthcoming need. "Are you sick?" I asked.

"I don't know," she said, twisting a lock of hair and sounding worried.

"Hungover?" I asked. The staff at these summer programs tended to drink a lot.

"No, I'm not hungover. I don't know. I'm taking these antibiotics, and it says on the bottle that they may cause nausea, so maybe that's why." She was puppy-like, with mousy-brown hair and spastic energy combined with superior physical coordination. A week or two later, the program director would see her dancing around, hair and arms flying, with a fellow sorority sister who was also on staff, and mutter, "Dartmouth kids. They are the human equivalent of Labradors."

I asked this girl, Sarah, if she had eaten anything yet today, and she said no. I had some scones my mother had packed for me after the funeral services. "You should get something in your stomach," I said, offering her a scone in a folded paper napkin. "Eat this and see if you feel better."

Sarah needed a caretaker, and I was up for the job. It was the perfect way to defer my own anxieties. And there was chemistry. Before long, Sarah and I were staring at each other across staff meetings, inventing reasons to work on projects together, having long talks after check-in—often about her last tumultuous relationship, with a girl—and eventually sneaking into each other's rooms to make out.

My crush made sense to no one, including her and me. During my own collegiate years at Brown, I edited a feminist magazine, dined in the smoking section of the cafeteria, and read Andrea Dworkin and Michel Foucault. Sarah, a rising senior at Dartmouth, played team sports, went to "drink-ups," and lived in a sorority house. Our incompatibility was good for a high drama quotient. Every week there were tears, conflicts, and declarations of crazy, impossible love. All of this contributed, of course, to a spectacular sex life.

Jomar and I split up with remarkably few bad feelings and continued to be close friends. Weekdays I introduced college undergraduates to Flannery O'Connor and the traditional model of the short story. Then I drove north and spent weekend nights in the basement of a sorority house, passing for a college student, playing dress-up, and drinking keg beer from a plastic cup. My friends thought I had lost my mind.

Indeed I had. And it was exhilarating. It felt amazing to prioritize nothing over the next high-emotion meeting with my new girlfriend. Nothing could have been more exotic to me than a basement full of beer-slugging, lesbian rugby players wearing baseball caps with the brims out sideways, who played beer pong all night only to get up and act like scholars in the morning. I simultaneously discovered the good gay life in Boston, which—I had no idea—was bursting with fun people who liked to dance, drink, stay up late, and spend weekends in the artists' beach mecca of Provincetown (how had I not yet discovered Provincetown?)—none of whom had children or mortgages in their twenties. The literary community in Boston was everything I thought a community should be, and I loved teaching at Emerson. I rented an apartment in the South End and started to call Boston home.

When Sarah struggled out of the binds of our relationship in what I considered a most cowardly fashion—drunken cheating, of course—I did what I often did when I needed to escape my life: I cruised the Internet for plane tickets and places to stay. I'd been curious about Nicaragua for years. Maybe I'd still need some help from Tylenol PM to close down my brain at night, but when I woke up in the morning the details of an exotic elsewhere would rush to fill my sensory receptors, and, ideally, I wouldn't be able to entertain ideas about anything outside of my current neighborhood on the planet.

As far as Sarah's side of the story went after our breakup, which was only our first breakup, I gave it little consideration. At the time, my side of the story was that she was selfish and heartless, and I was sticking to it.

But I didn't come to Nicaragua to think about all this.

Marla got serious about the past subjunctive. She drilled me all morning. By ten thirty, I was exhausted, with all kinds of past doubts in my head. I went into the office to refill my water bottle from the cooler. Diego was there, looking through an English textbook. Kristian was out in the courtyard, writing something in a spiral note-book and thinking hard about something. He was probably working with the present tense or simple past.

"Hi," Diego said, brightening. I miss you, I wanted to say, but I didn't know Diego well enough to say this to him.

"How are your classes?" he asked. His straight black hair fell into his eyes.

"They're fine." But I wish they were with you. "How are things going with the German?"

"Oh, fine." He smiled, professionally. "Have you seen the mural, the one with Che? Has Marla taken you to see the Sandinista art around the city?"

"We went to the zoo yesterday," I said. "It was interesting." Diego looked frustrated. "So," I said, "do you really think the Sandinistas have a chance in this election?"

"I think so," Diego said, "but people forget things very quickly. The people in the campo don't forget things as quickly as the people in the cities do. Literacy and health care are so much better there because of the Sandinistas." We smiled at each other. "I have some books for you," Diego said. We haggled; Diego tried to give me three books for no money, then finally let me pay him.

At home that afternoon, Doña Martha invited her friend César over to speak English with me, but as soon as I mentioned my trip to the zoo, Doña Martha had a few things to offer in Spanish.

"I was never a Somocista," Doña Martha said, referring to the truly evil dictator who had led Nicaragua before the Sandinistas took power. When the earthquake devastated Managua in 1972, Somoza took the blood donated by the Red Cross and sold it for his own personal gain. That act was fairly emblematic of his politics. "But that zoo is a tragedy of the Sandinistas. They built it and then abandoned it, and now the animals are left to suffer in cages."

Miguelito swept the floor near the bedrooms.

"I'm Somocista!" called Miguelito.

"No, you're not," Doña Martha said. "You're anti-Sandinista."

"I'm anti-Sandinista!" Miguelito said.

"See?" Doña Martha said. "Even Miguelito doesn't like the Sandinistas. And he doesn't even care about toothpaste! He didn't have toothpaste then and he doesn't have toothpaste now!" She cracked up.

César sipped at his coffee, looking grave.

"It sucked," César said in English.

Because I craved peace over conflict, I got friendly with Kristian. Marla and some of her girlfriends took us to the beach and sat drinking sodas while Kristian and I climbed waves and took pictures of each other turning cartwheels on the sand. Diego didn't come on field trips like this one. It seemed like too frivolous a thing for Diego to do.

I continued to see him at the school, but his looks lingered on me less and less. He was moving on, thinking about newer students and bigger things. Later in the year, when I was back in the States, Nicaraguan elections were held, and the Sandinistas lost. I imagined Diego's face when I read the news, his deflated sad eyes staring down at a volume of revolutionary poetry. And then I pictured Doña Martha hugging Miguelito, hugging Yasito, hugging her children and her own chest, and Marla breathing a sigh of relief for deodorant and toothpaste.

Like the Sandinista party, Sarah and I denied our defeat. After a pause of almost a year, we would try again, and for a while it seemed like it could pass for a stable, sensible relationship. But the desire to delay my own maturity was not a permanent condition. When I visited my friends in their late twenties with children, our conversations poking in around their children's endless needs, I felt no envy—only dread. But as our relationship stretched into my thirties, I would evolve toward wanting a commitment and a future, and Sarah was where I had been years before. Our breakup would be untidy and it would take me quite a long time to accept the fact that she preferred the freedom of the unknown over me.

"You knew how the story would go," Jomar consoled me over the phone. He had since moved back to New York, and had gone through his own series of dramatic relationships.

"I know," I said.

When clarity about my own situation eluded me, I was grateful to the places in the world like Nicaragua for letting me be involved in their stories, the stories that were bigger than the pit in my stomach and the insomnia from my past doubts and *if onlys* and the personal drama of wishing things were different than they were.

THE ANSWER WAS NO
(Cuba)

My friend Tim, codirector of Putney Student Travel, was skilled at talking me into things. This time he had spearheaded a program for American high school students in Cuba. Putney had finagled a license from the US Treasury. In the early 2000s I didn't know one could do such a thing, but apparently "education" was one of the ways Americans could legally get around the anti-Castro travel ban. They needed someone to teach writing and literature, so Tim called me. My answer was yes. I went to Cuba three summers in a row, five weeks at a stretch, and twice more to do program planning, always legally. From my first day on the job, I worked with a Cuban named Darwin.

My first time getting around the system in order to get into Cuba was the summer of 2001: just around the time that Darwin began trying to get *out* of Cuba. Darwin worked year-round in tourism, earning dollars illegally, and between jobs he fought for the paperwork to move to Spain. We worked together for June and July of that year, and in August I went back to the States; he was still where I left him when I came back to Cuba the following June to work again. For me, being in Cuba, though my job occupied me around the clock, was like a holiday. I had gifted students, and I had someone else's dollars to spend so I could use them to visit Hemingway's house, or to learn Afro-Cuban drumming techniques from a street musician, or to drink coffee at the Hotel Nacional and talk about books. Darwin did the dirty work for us. He had connections, and he made deals with bus drivers so we could travel economically, or introduced us to friends who would perform Santeria ceremonies or teach us salsa for cheap.

When I got back to Cuba in the summer of 2002, Darwin didn't look well. His body, as before, was solid: he was shorter than I was, which is to say below the height of the average American woman, and his arms and back were sturdy and masculine, his trunk square and muscled. He was not lacking a slight paunch. A wild head of curly, unruly hair that fell almost to his shoulders gave Darwin an animal virility. But his complexion was different from the last time I'd seen him. His sun-darkened, freckled skin was ashen, glossed with a sheen of sweat. He hacked a constant cough. His facial expressions betrayed the status of the invisible aspects of his health: he frequently had the fixed, pinched expression of a man withstanding something.

"It's my stomach," he said. "The doctors are saying no more caffeine."

That was horrible news. When Darwin and I had time to relax, it was always over espressos at the hotel bar.

"Or cigarettes, or alcohol, and many kinds of food, especially greasy food."

But the program we worked for was such that food was available in abundance—though, in Cuba, even wealthy Americans had limited menu choices, and most of the time these foods we ate were greasy— fried chicken and pizza without tomato sauce and spaghetti served in a shallow puddle of oil—and Darwin ate what we ate. It was understood that when we weren't there, Darwin, like most Cubans, was not precisely sure where his next meal would come from. You didn't turn down a month's worth of free food. You ate what you were served.

"The stress is not helping my situation," Darwin said. Every time he went to Migración to check on his paperwork, the officials smirked and told him the man he needed to see wasn't in. The officials knew who he was, knew that he worked illegally and that he lived in an illegal apartment. They had no desire to help him get out of Cuba. Even his relatives were deliberately making things difficult. One aunt in particular had it in for Darwin, had gone out of her way to rat on him when the officials stopped by her house to ask if Darwin resided in the house where he was registered. She felt Darwin thought he was better than the rest of them. (I had a feeling that he *did* feel this way. He worked hard; he refused to sit back and accept his lot.) Darwin felt ganged up on, straitjacketed. He had a quick temper, but exploding in Migración wasn't going to get him anywhere.

He stood coughing in the office where I was stationed with Sarah, another American, who'd been living in Cuba for three years. Sarah spoke Spanish with the most fantastic Cuban drawl and had fully integrated into La Habana life. She had known Darwin longer than I had and was impatient with his cough.

"Go to the doctor, Darwin," Sarah said, not looking up from the construction paper she was cutting with child-proof scissors.

"I'll go."

"Yeah, you keep saying that."

"I'll go!" Darwin sighed and shifted his backpack from his shoulder to the floor. He leaned over the desk to address me alone. "Are we going to have lunch today, Alden—just you and me?"

I raised an eyebrow. "You know what's going to happen if we go to lunch, just you and me," I said.

Darwin's posture was deflated. He was relenting to me. Darwin, my now dear friend, was a proud man with a fuck-you countenance that flared up whenever he was challenged. I'd been challenging him on this one thing since I'd met him.

I wanted him to tell me about Angola.

"I don't care. I feel like I could talk about Angola today." I'd been waiting for this day, the day Darwin would finally spill, since the day I'd seen the space suit in the Museo de la Revolución.

When Darwin was a young man, his mother, a fervent socialist, had enrolled him in a military high school. Darwin, at nineteen, had trained at the base in Guantánamo on the eastern coast of Cuba, and, after six months, boarded a plane with his fellow soldiers-in-training to go back to Havana. The flight time across the island was forty-five minutes. After an hour in the air, Darwin and the others were told they were not going to Havana after all. They were flying farther east, to Angola, to fight in their civil war.

Darwin was in Angola for two years. For months after he boarded that plane, his mother had no idea where he was.

That was the extent of what I knew.

I shut down my computer and closed it, leaving Sarah to her construction paper and scissors.

"Let's go to lunch," I said to Darwin. Slowly, he bent down to the floor and picked up his backpack by a strap.

We first came to Cuba, a year before this, in the middle of the hot season. We came with cotton T-shirts, with sleeves that we learned to push up onto our shoulders, and we learned to politely ignore the sweat stains that darkened each other's armpits. We came with a gang of American teenagers and a mission to teach them about a place about which we knew little. I left Boston with two guidebooks, a copy of *The Old Man and the Sea*, and some novels that would have been taken away from me if I'd been searched in Havana customs: *Dirty Havana Trilogy, Before Night Falls.* I was ignorant of the fact that these books were banned in Cuba. I was ignorant of many things: Angola, for instance. The only thing I knew about Angola was that it was a country in Africa, below the Congo, the heart of darkness.

My body was outraged by the heat, and I spent my first day in Cuba in a mild stupor. But I was already in love with Cuba. It was a blurry, yearning kind of love. Everything about Cuba confused me. Even the Spanish was almost impossible to understand; in other countries, I communicated almost as well as I did in English, but here, they had their own language, their *cubanismos*, and I was swamped with an unusually keen craving to understand what was going on around me. How did that boy with the ripped T-shirt and filthy knees have a shiny silver scooter? How was there a Benetton store in the Plaza Vieja—who shopped there? Was it possible, as an American, to befriend a Cuban on any level of equality?

I wore a thin, cotton skirt, and my thighs chafed as I walked through Old Havana. I watched Darwin as he walked ahead of me and flirted with another American teacher, a sour girl named Heather. I was jealous, not because I was attracted to Darwin (I wasn't) or because I didn't like Heather (I didn't), but because he was the only Cuban I had met in Cuba and on this day he was everything to me, more than the crumbling facades of the colonial buildings, the hallucinatory parade of midcentury American cars, or the overheard strings of Cuban Spanish dialect I strained to comprehend. I wanted Darwin to be talking to me.

In the Museo de la Revolución, Darwin found me standing in front of an old space suit with Russian writing on the front pocket. The space suit was a bizarre installation in a museum that contained mainly relics from the Cuban Revolution: bullets that had been shot in 1959, plaques explaining the heroics of Che Guevara, the extent of

Che's asthma, and the fact that he fought through it. The empty space suit sat on a chair in the middle of the room. The chair was old and wooden, one I'd expect to see in a grade-school classroom. It did not lend a sense of dignity to the slouching space suit.

"The space suit worn by the first Cuban to go into space," Darwin said in perfect English. "He went with a Russian team. They say he only got one order the whole time he was up there. You know what it was?"

I turned to face Darwin. He wore a tight, tie-dyed T-shirt and khaki pants rolled up to midcalf, and seemed unfazed by the heat. His eyes were alive and his movements were fluid and easy.

"What?"

"'Don't touch anything.'" Darwin snickered, and something about the way he did this, as a deliberate punctuation to his comment, reminded me that he often worked with American travelers in Cuba. He was a seasoned tour guide, and he knew which jokes would fly. He had a repertoire.

"*Ay, Cuba*," Darwin said. This was something all Cubans said, a tic of resignation, a what-can-you-do. I would start to say it soon. As I made my way into the next room of the museum, Darwin followed. We walked together from room to room and then, together, we walked out the door into the blinding heat of Havana.

The pastels of building fronts and repainted old cars bled into a deceptively cheerful rainbow. I began to feel less lethargic. Darwin walked by my side, between my body and the road, a position of protective masculinity. I didn't need Darwin to protect me; I normally had no problem deflecting strangers who approached me. But I ceded the position. Perhaps Darwin was protecting me from a threat of which I remained unaware. Or perhaps he just needed to feel that he was.

"The *jineteros* are everywhere," Darwin warned. "The hustlers. Preying on foreign tourists. Especially here in Old Havana. The best thing to do is ignore them."

"How did your English get so fluent?" I asked.

"From school. Watching movies. Working with Americans like you."

"Have you ever left the country?" I asked. I assumed he'd been abroad somewhere where English was the primary language.

"Once. I went to Angola."

"Why *Angola?*"

Nothing in Darwin's demeanor changed. He walked on, looking ahead of us, expressionless. Sweat ran down past his ears. I became self-conscious of the flop-flop sound my messenger bag made with each step as Darwin briefly halted the conversation. Then he told me about the war.

"I spent two years there in Angola, but when I came back I was one hundred years old."

I changed the subject out of nervousness. "Have you been any-where else?" Darwin was used to American ignorance. He was asked this question all the time. Americans knew about the Cuban missile crisis and they knew about Fidel Castro and they knew they were not supposed to be in Cuba, but you couldn't count on them to know that Cubans were rarely allowed out of the country. Even Darwin was not eligible for a passport, though he had been abroad before.

The answer was no.

Sarah stayed in the office to man the phones, in case someone called and needed something. This year, instead of teaching, I was program director. This meant I spent less time with the American high school students and more time with Darwin and the administration team. We spent hours on end in the office, sitting by the phone, waiting for someone to need us.

Darwin and I decided on lunch at the Rincón de Criollo restaurant, down the street from the hotel. Our other options in the neighborhood were the Italian restaurant and the Toro steak house, tourist restaurants owned by the same government chain as the Rincón de Criollo. The Italian restaurant listed mozzarella and tomato salads on the menu, though it was understood that mozzarella was one of those things you would never, ever find in Cuba, and we had gotten our fill of the greasy pizza with the mysterious, cheddar-tasting cheese that we almost always resorted to ordering. The Toro served unlimited roast beef, veal, lamb, and thick cuts of chewy steak. The Cuban government controlled the beef industry—in Cuba the jail sentence for killing a cow was longer than that for killing a human being—and the Toro was a mystery of indulgence, and very expensive. I always preferred the Rincón.

Darwin ordered the chicken soup and the roasted chicken. I ordered my usual: *arroz a la Cubana*, a small dish of rice and two fried, runny eggs, black beans, and lemonade. Darwin's soup came first. There was a fatty piece of goosepimpled chicken skin floating on top of the bowl, which was not uncommon and was the reason I didn't order chicken soup. I wondered if Darwin would eat it or put it on the side of his dish; he seemed to be eating around it. I wouldn't have eaten it.

I made my utensils dance a few steps of salsa. Knife was more graceful at this than Fork.

"I hope they have flan for dessert," I said. I didn't know where to start. Every time I had asked Darwin about Angola, I was greeted with an averted gaze and the feeling that I'd overstepped my bounds.

I thought of Darwin as a friend I would have for life. I'd told him things I hadn't discussed with anyone else on the staff. Darwin never judged.

"You are my sister," he said when I told him secrets.

Darwin had told me about his relationship with his Spanish wife, Chus, whom he'd married two months earlier; it was understood that he'd married her on some level to get out of Cuba. He'd told me about the times he'd been harassed by the police, when they'd tried to force him to spy on the Americans he worked for—us included. (He did. He spied on us and reported our activities, down to the films we watched, to the government; they made it impossible for him to continue working with us if he didn't. Eventually he told me that too.) He'd told me about the time last summer when Heather had come to his Havana apartment and, without a word, climbed into his bed, despite the fact that both of them were engaged at the time and she was supposed to be at the hotel, keeping tabs on the American teenagers who were in our care. (I punched him in the arm. Twice. "Her? *I can't believe you!*" Darwin cackled hysterically for a good five minutes.) Angola was the one conversation he seemed unwilling to have. On a completely selfish level, I was hurt by this. I wanted to remove the barrier, wanted Darwin to feel safe with me. I'll admit also that my curiosity was colored by morbidity. I was born one year before America withdrew from the war in Vietnam; I'd never known a peer who had been involved so deeply in war, and I wanted, quite simply, to know what Darwin had done.

"Well, it was a war that was going on forever," Darwin said. "It was Fidel's secret war, the Cuban Vietnam."

I'd spent the year between my summers in Cuba researching Angola because of Darwin. Angola gained independence from Portugal in 1975, when Darwin was four. Since then there had been nonstop civil war. The MPLA had communist leanings and was supported by Cuba. The United States, predictably, supported all parties that opposed the commies, and UNITA, an "Africanist" movement with emphasis on ethnic and rural rights, arose to become the MPLA's primary opponent. The powers of the world got busy. Machinery and vehicles and weapons rained down on Angola. Soldiers on both sides learned fragments of foreign languages from what was printed on the bodies of planes and boxes of medical supplies. Soldiers were imported like firearms, a gift of support from afar.

America's war in Vietnam had just ended, and Americans were not about to support involvement in another civil war on the other side of the world. Fidel recognized that Cuba could gain an international reputation by getting involved in the war in Angola and the United States wouldn't step in. So Cuba sent troops, and kept sending troops. As in Vietnam, the war in Angola showed no signs of ending, and no one seemed to be winning. In twenty-five years, more than half a million people were killed.

Cuba agreed to withdraw its troops in 1988, after much protest against the war within Cuba, when Darwin was eighteen years old. It was the year before Darwin boarded that plane.

"The war was supposed to be over," Darwin said. "When we were in Guantánamo, there was supposedly no more sending Cubans to Angola. It never occurred to us while we were in training that we'd be sent to fight."

I didn't understand. "How could they do that?"

Something also new to me this summer was Darwin's resigned, bitter grin. "Your uncle," Darwin said, pulling at his chin—the silent signal for Fidel—"does whatever he wants." Darwin's bowl was empty of liquid. He picked up the fatty piece of chicken and began sucking on the skin.

"Your uncle is driving me crazy," Darwin said. He laughed indulgently and I laughed with him. He'd taught me all the ways Cubans talked around the topic of Fidel. He was Your Uncle, he was My Friend, he was *Comandante*, he was *El Caballo*, he was *Numero Uno*. He was the act of tugging at your imaginary beard. Darwin loved being the one to teach me these things.

"One guy, he tried to kill himself on the plane," Darwin said. "He tried to cut his wrists with a piece of metal."

My *arroz a la Cubana* came and I made a bed for the black beans from my pile of rice. The eggs were viciously salted and after three bites my lips and tongue began to feel numb. Darwin's plate of roasted chicken was placed to the side, to give him time to finish his soup.

"Did you kill anyone?" I asked Darwin.

"Of course I did, Alden." I looked down at his soup bowl and dish and there was nothing left but bones.

When Darwin was about three bites into his roasted chicken, the details began to come out in a flood. He put down his fork. My eggs were gone and my tongue was swollen inside my mouth.

"I was on the plane with four of my good friends from home. We were all land mine diffusers. Three of my friends died fourteen days after arriving. Twenty of us died that day. In the beginning we were three hundred something; in the end, two years later, we were one hundred and seventy-five."

On Guantánamo they learned bush survival. Their two years in Angola were spent entirely in the jungle.

"I was a specialist on defusing, fusing, planting, and mining bombs," Darwin said. "I should have died . . . *many* times."

After twenty-five years of war, Angola had the most mines on the planet. Angola has more amputees from land mines than any other country in the world. Millions of mines were there still, waiting to be disarmed, driven over, stepped on. In Havana, if you see a man without an arm or missing both his legs, ask him if he's ever traveled outside of Cuba.

"That was how my three friends died when we were first there. We were driving north in military trucks. One second they were up in the truck ahead of me, the next there was an explosion. They'd driven over a mine."

"And they were land mine diffusers," I said, but as soon as I said it, I realized that in the midst of that many land mines, the irony wasn't that acute.

"But do you know what bothered me more sometimes than people dying from mines? When people died for no reason at all."

"What do you mean?"

"One time, for fun, someone shot a hyena and killed it. A male. Sixty-five kilometers later, another hyena attacked. She followed us the whole way up the road. A female."

Let's say it was a spotted hyena. The females are larger than the males, and both have phalluses of the same size; the females dominate. The young try to kill each other literally minutes out of the womb: two cubs will fight each other until they see the mother licking down the fur of a third, at which point they both attack the third and try to kill it. Hyenas are the only mammals born with their eyes open and their teeth in working order. Top speed for hyenas is thirty-seven miles per hour, and they can take down a wildebeest three times their weight. They are not the cowering foragers they arc reputed to be. Some animals are just born mean.

Female spotted hyenas mate with males outside their clan. They mate once and move on. They do not form attachments. Sorrow over the death of her mate does not explain why that female hyena attacked Darwin's troop that day. Perhaps it was sheer outrage in the face of a frivolous threat.

The hyena killed the man she attacked, shredded flesh with her teeth, while the rest of them watched and clamored for their guns.

"Why?" Darwin said. "For nothing."

Another time, while crossing a river, someone in Darwin's troop shot an elephant.

"For fun," Darwin said. "Just because. Only, he didn't kill the elephant. He only shot him in the leg. Elephant charges, attacks one of the trucks. Four people die."

Darwin's words had picked up speed. There was more anger in them than sorrow.

"Why? Why?" Darwin threw up his hands.

I had seen Darwin in a rage, red faced, an elastic band pulled tight and ready for release, and I had seen Darwin reel it in and force the color from his face. I'd seen it emerge more than once, often when it was not appropriate.

There were a few things that consistently caused Darwin to lose his cool, among them: *jineteros* who targeted his foreign friends looking for cash; men hitting on his female friends, primarily Cuban men hitting on his foreign female friends; and the sight or subject of Cuban officials, primarily police officers, whom he considered to be the stupidest people on earth.

"They're dumb kids from the country who don't know any better," Darwin said of the police officers. "Most of them can't write. When we pass the military academy, we say, 'Look, it's the school where you go in stupid and come out an imbecile!'"

"What about the Ministerio people," I said, knowing he couldn't dismiss the higher-ups in the same fashion. The Ministerio people had real power over him. They made *decisions*. Police officers, in Darwin's mind, were the government's hired thugs.

Darwin pulled his cotton headband off his head and then back on, using it to absorb forehead sweat along the way.

"Sometimes I think they're never going to let me out of this fucking place," Darwin said.

It was not just pain in his stomach that had turned Darwin's expression sour. It was this new sense of helplessness, of being stuck in Cuba. Chus had flown to Cuba from Spain early when the fiancé visa they'd applied for was stalled. They'd wed at Havana's equivalent of the courthouse, without thrown rice, without a white dress, without family, without ceremony. They'd done what they were supposed to do. Chus flew back to Spain to attend to her pharmacy job and her ailing parents, and Darwin was left waiting for someone to slide his papers out from under their virtual paperweight, where they gathered dust, legal, save the signatures of the officials who didn't feel they owed this renegade, dollar-earning, illegal tour guide any favors. He was doing fine getting around the system. Why should the system help him?

"I feel like I'm dying here," Darwin said, which made me wonder if he meant: "I'm afraid I might die here."

But no, that wasn't the case. Darwin was a fighter, and a finagler. He'd get what he wanted. It was the waiting that killed him, and the wondering if he should try some other way.

I'd seen Darwin tense and then explode with anger when no one saw it coming. He'd once narrowly averted getting into an exchange of blows at a dance party with a Cuban whom he suspected was trying to dance too close to our female students. Darwin let him have it, got in his face, then instructed the students, along with their teacher, to leave the club, resulting in a loud argument outside of the club with the teacher, who hadn't wanted to leave, and who didn't appreciate Darwin's machismo.

"We were all fine," the teacher said later. "The kid was sketchy, but it was under control. Darwin just flipped."

More than any other subject, the officials who prevented him from leaving Cuba—and Fidel was counted among them—were the inspiration for Darwin's fits of anger.

"I hate them," Darwin said. His mouth tightened as if drawn by string. "Sometimes, I swear to you, if I had the resources . . ."

Darwin mimed the act of dropping a bomb. With his mouth, he made it explode.

I tried not to dwell on the fact that Darwin's stress had cost him the pleasure of coffee. I quietly ordered a café Cubano and asked the waitress if there was any flan.

The food in Cuba was uniformly terrible, with few exceptions, and one of these exceptions was flan.

"Sorry, no flan today." The waitress tilted her head apologetically in reaction to my jaw-drop of devastation.

I pathetically asked the waitress, "Are you *positive* there isn't any flan?" It wasn't uncommon, in Cuba, to make an authoritative statement without possessing the proper evidence. The waitress reemerged from the kitchen carrying a small plate with two adorable, delectable little custards quivering under their caramel sauce.

I exclaimed gracias a few more times than necessary to show my gratitude, and the waitress smiled girlishly, immensely pleased that she'd been able to do this for me.

"You have a flan problem," Darwin said.

"We know this," I said.

"You are addicted to flan."

"Are you planning to eat yours or what?"

Darwin pushed his plate across the table toward me, smirking. Decadence was part of both our personalities, and it was strange to see him adhere to a regimen that denied him such things. I was floored that he'd been able to give up beer, another of our shared pleasures; he told me, "If I start drinking beer again it will be like giving up after all this sacrifice."

"Terrible," I said, pointing my spoon at the flan.

"I blew up a bridge once," Darwin said. "There were trucks on it and I pressed the button and blew it up." Darwin must have seen, and predicted, some of the discomfort I felt about knowing this side of him. He owned it. "Sometimes," he said, "even still, when somebody makes me mad, I look at them and I think, 'I could kill you.' Because I really could. Once I had a gun, and all I had to do was reach in my pocket."

"Have you done anything violent since you came home?"

"There were some guys who once broke into my friend Andrea's apartment during the Special Period and stole some food," Darwin said. The Special Period was Fidel's euphemism for the years following the collapse of the Soviet Union, when almost everyone in Cuba went hungry. Raft building reached new levels of creativity during the Special Period.

"Andrea had some malanga. It was all we had to eat and they broke in while we were right there in the kitchen, and took it from us. Alden, we had literally nothing to eat."

I was on my second flan now. I was barely leaving traces of caramel sauce on the plate. I was obscene. I thought, *Someone should stop me.*

"Back then they used to make these glass yogurt jars. I took four of those and I made molotov cocktails. I had four of them in my closet. And I was going to use them. They are like little bombs. My friend, one of my friends who was also in Angola, opened my closet and he saw them. He asked me what they were and I lied, but he knew. He said, 'You have to get rid of these. You can't use them.' He saved me.

"People save each other," Darwin said. "People who've taught me where to put my anger, how to direct it, they've saved me."

Darwin and I started back to the hotel, walking close to the buildings where there was shade. The sidewalk between Rincón and the hotel was made of slippery tiles. There was one spot where I'd seen countless people slide and lose their footing, and where I'd almost fallen down more than once. Just after we cleared this slickest spot, Darwin caught his shoe on some obstacle on the sidewalk and fell down face first, catching himself by one hand with an audible *smack*.

It was a hard fall, but it was not a disastrous fall. Darwin picked himself up and said, "That was close." I knew I should try to make him laugh, but this time, I couldn't. I felt it in my stomach, the damage that was undoable. My wait, the wait for Darwin to tell me this part of his history, was over, but I carried the suspense of Darwin's wait to emigrate.

I thought that if Darwin was finally able to get out of Cuba, his stomach might unclench. Darwin was as trapped now as he was in Angola. The only time he'd been allowed out of the country, the one thing he wanted now, was the worst thing that had happened to him.

Ay, Cuba.

As long as I had a job I would come back to Cuba. I was stuck in my own way, but my version of stuck was an absurdly luxurious choice. One of the things for which I was most grateful to Darwin was that he never resented me for the luxuries I'd been gifted at birth; he didn't want me to feel guilty for the freedoms I enjoyed, but he couldn't stop me from that.

Just being here, in my case, was an act of defiance, and I'd done it so easily. The US government didn't want me to come to Cuba? They couldn't stop me! I'd even done it legally, and had a wad of dollars shoved in my pocket to spread around the country, so a bunch of Americans could have fun.

In Darwin's shoes, I might have resented all of us for this. But Darwin saw us and merely wanted the same privileges—to stay in the same hotels, to walk the same beaches without getting harassed by police, and to make money doing a job because he was good at it.

"Do you think you'll make it to Spain soon?" I asked.

Darwin looked at me wearily and gave no answer.

The next year, I came back to work for a third summer. I exited the Havana airport to the barrage of billboards advertising peace, unity, and socialism. Darwin stood in the sun waiting for me, holding a sweating Bucanero beer for me in one hand, a Bucanero for himself in the other. He did some goofy dance steps and raised the beer cans high.

Despite myself, I was more glad to see his kinky hair, his beer-wet lips, his tie-dyed shirt and smile—here, under the pounding Cuban summer sun—than I was anything.

THIS IS NOT A CRUISE
(Around the World)

I could not get used to the windows in Classroom 3. They ran from floor to ceiling, lining the entire portside wall. The Pacific Ocean rolled by. Later, in other seas, there would suddenly be land when we weren't expecting to see land, or The Voice would come over the speakers—"Goooood morning, everyone. If you are starboard, you might catch a glimpse of sea turtles swimming alongside the ship"—and we'd all have to stop what we were doing to run and see for ourselves. After a week, the students had gotten better about not staring out at the wavering horizon; I still found those windows distracting.

"Help me close the shades," I said, and began to lower the shade closest to the podium. There was a collective groan. "Sorry," I said. "We're looking at a Powerpoint today."

I powered up the overhead projector. The ship rocked. I clutched at the podium. The first time my balance faltered, students laughed; now it was just your standard, daily ship-rocking.

I led a discussion on the paintings of Paul Gauguin. "What do you make of Gauguin's use of flatness and unrealistic color?"

"He's exaggerating the primitiveness of Tahitian culture."

"He's trying to reclaim the innocence of the primitive people."

"What do you make of this slide? Would this positioning of bodies have been acceptable if Gauguin had used naked French women as models instead of the Tahitian women represented here?"

"Professor? We can't really see."

I walked in front of the podium and turned to face the screen. All the eye could make out were vague shadows of color. The sun was too bright; the shades couldn't keep it out. We did what we could to block it, but sunlight prevailed over the meek light of the projector.

"So, the world outside is interfering with our classroom studies. Does anyone see a metaphor here?"

We were on the fall '06 voyage of Semester at Sea. I was one of three English professors. I taught three classes on the *MV Explorer*: creative writing, travel writing, and a literature course designed for a group of college students who happened to be going around the world, Exoticism in Literature. It was a variation of a course I had developed at my home institution; I had now taught five sections of Exoticism in Literature and Art as a first-year seminar at Emerson College.

As with many of my jobs teaching abroad, the offer of a position as a professor on Semester at Sea had stunned me. Four years earlier, I filled out a two-page application I'd downloaded from the Internet, attached my CV, and heard nothing for over two years. I had almost forgotten I'd applied until an e-mail arrived in my in-box from Fil Hearn, the academic dean for the fall '06 voyage. The e-mail read simply, "How would you like to bc considered for a position as Visiting Lecturer on Semester at Sea? The itinerary is as follows: San Diego, Hawaii, Japan, China, Hong Kong, Vietnam, Cambodia, Myanmar, India, Turkey, Egypt, Croatia, Spain, Ft. Lauderdale." I stared at the screen of my laptop in disbelief.

The position was like a big fat peace offering from the universe after one of the most disagreeable years of my life.

First there was the inevitable final break with Sarah and the subsequent collapse of our cozy friend group. Then, at my friend Valerie's wedding, in which I was a bridesmaid, I slipped while walking down a grassy hill in flip-flops. My right foot dragged along the grass and popped out of its socket, and when I put weight down to reclaim my balance, the ball joint jammed between my tibia and fibula, causing the fibula to crack. When I looked down, my foot appeared to be on backward. The ambulance drove divots in Valerie's parents' back lawn and I was loaded onto a stretcher. Two operations later, I spent the end of summer on my parents' couch with my leg elevated, swallowing Percocets and watching *Buffy the Vampire Slayer* by the season. The time it took my leg, ankle, and foot to heal—I was off crutches quickly, but I limped for much longer than seemed reasonable—reflected my mental state. I couldn't locate my lost spirit, and I couldn't shake the fog. The one thing I managed to do well during this time was teach, and I was grateful for my career.

Professor Hearn interviewed me over the phone. "It was your Exoticism course that caught my eye," he said. He had come across my CV in a file of three years' worth of applications. "That seems like the perfect course for Semester at Sea." My course syllabi were approved and a contract was signed, but I didn't believe it was actually happening until I arrived in San Diego, my passport jammed with entrance visas.

By then I was feeling some of the buoyancy of my old self. It was hard to feel bad about life when you were about to go around the world on a ship.

Aaron lived in San Diego now, so I flew in early to spend a couple of nights with him and his wife, Annie. They took me out for my last meal on American land. We ate sushi with bamboo chopsticks and sipped sake from little cups.

"You should have an affair while you're on Semester at Sea," Aaron suggested. That sounded like a good idea to me.

"But with whom?" I said. "It's not like the odds are good for there being a hot, single, smart, fun gay lady on such a small staff," I said. I had a liberal dating policy when it came to gender, but my efforts over the past year proved my tendencies toward women were winning out.

"But there will be a lot of single *students*," Aaron suggested with a smirk. *Bad* idea.

I boarded the *MV Explorer* as one of sixty teachers and staff and 550 students. We came from colleges and universities all over the United States, from community colleges to Stanford. We traveled around the world with a top speed of twenty-eight knots. The ship was 590 feet long and weighed 24,300 tons. It was four years old, and it gleamed with fresh paint and the constant swabbing of the wooden decks.

"This is not a cruise," the deans reminded us, repeatedly. "This is a voyage of discovery."

Semester at Sea may not have been a cruise, but one thing was certain: we were on a cruise ship.

In one hundred days we sailed from San Diego to Florida, stopping for five days each in ten ports. Classes were held the days we were on the ship; while in port, we were free to travel as we pleased. Though it's safe to say the students did not sign up for Semester at Sea primarily for the academics, they were there to learn.

Back home, I'd designed my Exoticism course around books I liked, contemporary art I liked, and Orientalist art I'd researched because it was what most scholars identified with the word *exoticism*. As I defined it, as far as literature and art went, exoticism was *the representation of one culture for consumption by another culture*. Exoticism was Gauguin's painting scenes of Tahiti and showcasing his work for the French Academy, Gustave Flaubert's writing a tome about Egypt before he'd set foot there—in French, of course, for a French audience— and white American Norman Rush's writing fiction that took place in Africa and publishing it in the United States. The course had developed organically out of my own travel experiences and my writing about them.

It all started with a conversation I had at a party with a Dominican American writer whose work I admired. I had just returned from one of my trips to Costa Rica. A mutual friend had introduced us, thinking that between the Spanish–Latin America connection and our both being writers from New Jersey we might become friends. Plus there was the fact that I had an unsubtle crush on him, as many young female writers did at the time (and still do, I'm sure). When he asked me about my writing, I told him I had just finished work on two short stories that took place in Costa Rica.

We were standing over a bowl of Doritos. He eyed me, blond hair, Urban Outfitters fashion, with suspicion.

"Are you Costa Rican?" he asked. I told him I was not.

Later he went to the podium and read a story from his debut collection, which had just been published and was getting a lot of attention. Then he took questions from an audience made up of New York public high school students.

A student asked, "How do you maintain your voice in the white publishing industry?"

I stood in the back of the crowd. "It's funny," he said. "People always want to write *about* us. Like we're the fucking anthropological study of the month." I was fairly certain he was looking directly at me.

For weeks I could not bring myself to write.

Instead, I read. I read novels by Paul Bowles, Isak Dinesen, Joseph Conrad, and Melanie Sumner. Had they been doing something wrong by writing about cultures other than their own? It seemed that some of them were; Gustave Flaubert, in the letters he wrote home from Egypt, wrote about beatings of Egyptians as if it were the most fabulous variety of "local color," and passed off his own imagined Egypt as the real thing in *The Temptation of Saint Anthony*. But Paul Bowles, an American who eventually settled in Morocco, seemed to be doing it right; his characters faced their greatest feelings of alienation within their closest relationships, and American culture was not the yardstick by which North Africa was measured. There were models, indeed, for a "good" exoticism. Edward Saïd, the father of Orientalism, would likely have disagreed—in his opinion, all representations of the "East" by Western writers were erroneous—but I found solace in other theorists, especially French critic Tzvetan Todorov.

Yes, Todorov theorized, much old-school exoticism was ethnocentrism: the belief that one's own culture was superior to all others. The other side of the coin was primitivism. Paul Gauguin, champion of primitivism, fled France for the "superior" culture of Polynesia, where the people lived in harmony with nature and were free of the artificial codes of Western society. But Gauguin idealized Tahiti to such a degree that the people were reduced to what they represented, and he never truly unchained himself from the Western world; he was always, of course, hoping to sell his paintings in France. Ethnocentrism and primitivism both failed to consider the whole picture of a culture.

But say there was another way to see things. Say there was a way to logically consider what was good or bad in one's own culture as well as another. "We might try to at least imagine such a creature," Todorov suggested, of the nonethnocentric universalist, or humanist.

It seemed to me that the determining factor in being a "good" or "bad" exoticist was how far outside her own perspective a writer, or traveler, would venture. It mattered where they'd gone, why they'd gone, and how they got there. It boiled down to how one traveled.

On Semester at Sea, I went about using books to gently bully young college students into being responsible travelers. I believe that sometimes it worked. More than often, I was preaching to the converted. Some Semester at Sea students came on the trip to lie at the pool and get wasted in Kobe, Cairo, and Ho Chi Minh City. But most of them were here because they wanted to understand the world.

Exoticism in the American classroom was straightforward. Emerson students were more than happy to point out the pitfalls of primitivism in the work of Paul Gauguin. They were arts and communication majors, young writers and filmmakers and set designers and actors. They were critical, confident, and funny.

"Gauguin acts like he's all back to nature. He forgot to mention in *Noa, Noa* that all his food was canned stuff that came from a store."

"He married a fourteen-year-old and they couldn't even understand each other's languages! That's disgusting."

But it was easier to condemn this sort of behavior when one read *Noa, Noa* in one's dorm room in Boston. It might be more difficult to look down on the tourist who ate packaged food when you were in a village in India and had to choose between offending the woman who offered you milk straight from the cow and getting really, really sick.

It was complicated. I, for my part, entertained new debates between my inner Tourist and Traveler.

The Traveler could not believe I wanted to participate in such a phenomenon as Semester at Sea. Traveling around the world and stopping in ten countries just long enough to learn the words hello and thank you and promptly forget them. Residing, for three months, on a cruise ship with a pool and a spa, in a cabin with a porthole, a king-sized bed, marble bathroom floors, and two closets. And a cabin steward—Edwin, from the Philippines—who cleaned my cabin twice a day.

I even had an ice bucket. Who needed an ice bucket?

But Tourist looked at Traveler and shrugged, trying not to crack up. Was this guy kidding? Semester at Sea was the coolest thing ever!

It's not as if I was going to complain about going around the world on a ship. No one could argue that this wasn't a dreamy way to travel.

The question was how to change my lens so I could look at it as the *right* way to travel.

We stopped in Hawaii long enough to refuel. I led a trip to the Polynesian Cultural Center, which was like a Polynesian-themed Epcot Center run by Mormons. All the Hawaiian scenery I saw in Hawaii was fake. Other fake islands—Tahiti, the Marquesas, Samoa—surrounded a fake lake, and everywhere in between the "islands" were souvenir stands selling Hawaiian Barbie dolls, plastic leis, wooden masks, and woven hats.

I sat with my student Hilary and watched a Marquesan tribal dance performed by dancers wearing chemically dyed feather headdresses and carrying factory-made spears. The Marquesan MC coaxed four newly wedded men onto the Astroturf stage, handed them spears, and instructed them to "kill the pig." The tourists fake-stabbed at a teenage boy dressed in a pig costume made of dried grass and rope. They carried the dead "pig" away on a stake.

Now *this* was exoticism.

Hilary and I clapped and smiled.

"How exotic!"

"How charming!"

"They're so primitive! It's so genuine!"

"Gauguin would hate it here."

"Yes, he would, Hilary. Yes, he would."

For lunch we went to the Polynesian snack bar. We ate hot dogs and drank Diet Cokes.

Then we were back on the ship.

Climb the metal stairs. Spread your feet and arms apart, get frisked and wanded by security. Even your bra is on limits for the frisk. (Sneaky girls with small breasts borrowed the bras of their large-breasted friends, and lined the bras with plastic bags filled with booze.) Swipe your card in your cabin door, drop your bag, look for your friends, tell them your stories.

After Hawaii, the best stories going around were the ones about the students who got caught trying to smuggle alcohol onboard.

"So this kid brought on a case of water bottles, plastic wrap intact, and we almost let it get through. But then Chris—the security officer?—noticed that the lid on one of the bottles was a tiny bit askew."

"Vodka?"

"Yup."

"Busted!"

"Poor fools," my friend Brian, the ship videographer, said. He opened his backpack and produced a double-tall bottle of cheap white wine. We held out our cups.

Upstairs on Deck 7, in the faculty/staff lounge, Mag, from the Philippines, served up piña coladas and Tiger beer and bowls of cheddar-flavored Goldfish. Early on, the young and the childless gathered nightly to commune with potential friends and travel companions, and to occasionally get drunk and sing karaoke.

I was big on karaoke. My preferred karaoke song was "Crimson and Clover" in the style of Joan Jett, but that was not available on the ship's karaoke machine, so I resorted to Christina Aguilera's "Genie in a Bottle." Brian was a karaoke fan, and so was Kate, the twenty-eight-year-old head administrator and assistant to the executive dean. Kate's karaoke song was "Bette Davis Eyes." She sang it with in a deep-throated alto, with lots of gusto and usually a dance move or two.

I'd first noticed Kate during staff introductions when we were docked in San Diego. She stood at the podium and said, "I'm not sure exactly what my job is, but I'm sure you'll all help me figure it out," with an easy, liquid laugh and a comfort in her body I admired. She had short auburn hair that she kept pinned back with an elaborate network of bobby pins. It occurred to me that she was charming and magnetic and fun to be around, but it didn't occur to me that she was gay.

During the crossing from Hawaii to Japan we were at sea for ten days. It was the longest stretch we traveled without a port. Our group of friends found a quick intimacy during those nights we were "stuck" on the ship, and soon we were dishing about recent relationships.

I explained to Kate, "The last person I dated had a psychotic cat, and I have a neurotic dog, so we didn't stand much of a chance." In addition to using the word "person," I risked my reputation as an English professor by choosing the gender-neutral *they* over the singular *her*. It was exhausting to come out all the time when you looked as straight as I did, though my hair was chunked out at the time in bleached blond and candy apple red, which alluded to a detachment from the mainstream.

Kate said, "Just so you know, I mostly only date women," and grinned.

We both took quick sips of Tiger beer.

Kate's daytime post was at the center of the ship. When I passed through the central offices on my way to the dining hall, I caught glimpses of her half hidden behind her computer monitor, writing up the latest dean's memo, or laughing with her work-study students. When professors needed an exam copied or teaching supplies, they went through Kate.

Before we arrived in Japan I stopped by to request a dry-erase marker.

"Blue or black?" she asked.

"Either one will do."

"What are you doing in Japan?"

"I don't know, exactly," I told Kate. "I got a rail pass."

"Me too," she said, and lifted her hand for a high five.

Kate had studied abroad in Nicaragua and traveled extensively in Guatemala and Costa Rica. It was rare that I could talk about my time in Central America and not have to explain anything. Kate and I knew, from our shared attraction to the same places on the planet, that we would be good travel companions. But as for getting together? Oh, that would probably be a bad idea. One hundred days on a small ship would be a long time if something went awry.

Kate and I sometimes shared a chair in the faculty/staff lounge, even when two seats were free, but for now we were just, as she put it, "besties."

Days, we were busy. When there weren't classes, there were meetings. I spent my hour-long windows of free time on the elliptical machine at the gym, or grading papers in my cabin, wishing I could be sitting by the pool, on Deck 7 aft, among the students who rocked in the sun, watching the frothy wake of our ship fading into the horizon.

Then I figured out I could grade papers *at* the pool.

In Exoticism, we discussed Arthur Golden's novel, *Memoirs of a Geisha*, and the film adaptation of the novel.

"White, Western author, writing about a Japanese geisha. Being forced into prostitution worked out pretty well for this girl. Realistic?"

"I loved the movie," one student said.

"Me too!" several students said.

Ah, yes. Work to be done.

The ship cleared in Kobe and the Amazing Race began: the contest was judged on who could see the most and the best of Japan in five days. The stakes seemed high during this first port. No one wanted to miss the Best Thing, and no one had a surplus of time. We swiped our cards at the gangway, scattered. We were free of school obligations while in port.

In Japan, Kate and Brian and I spent a night at a ryokan on the island of Miyajima, wearing matching kimonos, eating delectable, unidentifiable foods in our own private dining room, and lounging in the baths. That night we drank sake, still in our kimonos, into the wee hours.

Brian guessed that I'd grown up on a hippie commune with free-spirit parents. I almost spit out my sake. "Sorry to disappoint you," I said. "I spent my youth at the Montclair Kimberley Academy, dressed in Laura Ashley."

I guessed that Kate, with her well-adjusted manner and easy happiness, had grown up with parents who were still madly in love, a few brothers, a golden retriever or a yellow lab, and summers on Martha's Vineyard. Kate almost spit out her sake. "Try single teenage mom on welfare," she said. Then I *did* spit out my sake.

Brian, the scruffy, anxious vagabond artist who'd settled in Portland, Oregon, revealed that he'd grown up in Georgia.

Kate and I looked at him quizzically, then said in unison, "*Georgia?*"

When you sail into the open sea with strangers, you leave your past behind.

We took a train to Kyoto and biked around the city. Here is a picture of the silver pagoda. Here is a picture of the gold pagoda. Here is a postcard from the Hiroshima Peace Memorial Museum. We spent two nights at a karaoke club and sang until our vocal chords betrayed us. The last morning, Brian woke up to find Kate and me sharing the narrow futon to his left while the futon to his right had been abandoned.

"So," he said, "this is how it's going to be for the rest of the trip, huh?"

Kate and I giggled, kissed. At least we had lasted until Japan.

Then we were back on the ship.

Climb the flimsy metal steps. Swipe your shipboard ID. Enter your private square of the ship, that safe bubble of comfort. The door clicks behind you.

Once the ship cleared in Kobe, and everyone was back onboard, The Voice came over the loud speaker. "Attention, everyone. There will be an emergency meeting in the Union at 2000 hours. All must attend."

We were having our first emergency!

A year earlier, the *Explorer* had been hit by a rogue wave while en route from Vancouver to Japan. It was a dramatic disaster. Windows were blown out; engines were disabled; glass tables and cabin mirrors shattered. Students and faculty were flown to Japan while the ship was repaired. This was not one of Semester at Sea's more reassuring legends.

But it was an *exciting* legend.

The eye of Typhoon Shanshan was rolling right at us. It had been on a path for Taiwan, then hooked toward Japan just before our departure. The *MV Explorer* was rerouting; we were skipping Qingdao, China, altogether, and going straight to Hong Kong. The ship pulled out the minute all shipboard IDs had been swiped. The crew put out baskets of Meclizine pills and soda crackers.

In bed, groggy from Meclizine, I stared at the ceiling as the sea lifted my bed, then dropped it. My stomach was in my throat. This was not fun at all. I hoped Kate, whose cabin was in the center of the ship, fared better than I did at the front of the ship. Something clattered behind the bathroom door. I rose, clawed at my bedclothes to keep from falling, and made it to the bathroom, where I removed from the sink my electric toothbrush, a bottle of hair-shine serum, and a glass pot of facial moisturizer that was somehow still intact. Everything went under the sink. The smack and thunder of the ship bucking on the water went on into the next day.

A third of the seats in my Exoticism class were empty. People were locked in their cabins, throwing up; some could not wake up from the Meclizine. Those who did attend my class looked stoned and took an exam, applying theory to an essay by Seth Stevenson called "Trying Really Hard to Like India."

"Sorry about this," I said, handing out the tests.

I bumped into walls. I knocked over a chair. In the lobby outside her office, Kate taught me how to get the timing right: when the ship pitches, you can jump into the air, and you'll stay there—you can fly.

I missed the Great Wall of China. I missed Tiananmen Square. I wasn't all that disappointed to miss these things. It was a big world.

In Southeast Asia something shifted. It was easy to *travel* in Vietnam or Cambodia or India, easier than it was in modernized cities like Hong Kong or Tokyo: people were more open, transportation systems were more chaotic, diseases were more infectious, and standard rules of behavior were more likely to go out the window.

Also, things were cheap.

In Ho Chi Minh City, the shuttle dropped us in front of the Hotel Rex, which we'd heard had been the hub for American GI leisure time during what we'd taken to calling "the American War." The market, blocks away, seemed like a logical place to start our explorations of Saigon. You say *market*, I think *lunch*.

Bartering fever diverted us. Street vendors, squatting on the sidewalk, used machetes to lop off the tops of green coconuts and offered us the whole thing with a straw. "One dollar!"

My instinct was to ignore them. But when we passed the third coconut vendor, already choking on Saigon heat and motorbike fumes, the juice started to look pretty good. Kate squatted down to meet a vendor, a teenage boy in a greasy trucker's hat, and attempted to trust him as he told her how much her dong was worth in dollars. He took her dong and we had our coconut.

"How much did you pay for that?" A Semester at Sea student coming the other way held his own coconut.

"A dollar."

"You could have gotten two for a dollar," he said.

Thirty minutes later I was lost in the maze of the indoor market, laden with plastic shopping bags. The original plan was to investigate the scene for later gift buying, eat lunch, then head into the city. But then my eyes fell on this adorable tea set, square black-and-turquoise cups with bamboo handles and a bamboo tray, for ten dollars. And then there was this silk bag I thought my sister would love—four dollars. The assistant dean, Roanne, rounded a corner and grabbed Kate by the sleeve. "You have to go to this stall," she said, handing her a wilted business card. "They have the best silk, everything fits!" We went to the stall, where I asked if they had anything in my size, gesturing to my American sized 8-10 body. "I think we have Extra,

Extra Large," the stall manager said. Shortly I owned an ankle-length red dress, a black dress with red tubing, a yellow side-button top, and three gift scarves. Silk. Well made. *Fancy.* Thirty-eight dollars for it all. These were unimaginable bargains!

As we were heading toward the exit, I stopped to examine a red, patent leather Gucci knockoff clasp purse. It was totally tacky, and though it was also fabulous, partially for its tackiness, I can't say I really wanted to own this bag.

"Ten dollar."

"Three dollars," I said automatically.

"No, no. Ten dollar. Good price."

We played it out. I walked away. The vendor yanked me back with a lower price. We two pretended to become insulted and annoyed with each other. I looked down, and in my hands was the purse, wrapped in tissue paper, and my wallet was seven dollars lighter. That's when I knew I had to stop.

Later, when we discussed Vietnam in the context of Tim O'Brien's war stories, I asked my Exoticism students: "What did you associate with Vietnam before you went there?"

"The war," they answered unanimously.

"And now?" I asked.

Silence.

"Shopping?" I asked.

Laughter, muttered assent.

"That's not what I associate it with," one student, not laughing, said. "I asked this guy if he would take me across the river in this little wooden boat. He brought me home to meet his family. I made friends in Vietnam."

Meanwhile, my creative writing students were beginning to generate some really impressive work. I told Brian and Andy in the faculty/staff lounge about a hilarious and tension-fraught essay one student, Tyler, had written about trying to get a massage in Vietnam *without* getting a hand job.

"That happened to me too," Brian said.

"That happened to me too," Andy said.

They were both visibly traumatized. "I don't want to talk about it," Andy said.

"Let's just say it was a battle until the end," Brian said.

Midsemester, each Exoticism student gave a presentation about how they traveled. The assignment was based on the categories of exoticism delineated by Todorov: ethnocentrism, primitivism, and humanism. We'd used these to examine the literary texts and the accompanying art; now we were turning it around on ourselves.

We'd read Flaubert, partly, to knock him down. We'd criticized the way he exploited his French power to gain access to important people in Egypt. We criticized the fact that the only women he connected with during his two years in Egypt were prostitutes. But we also watched him shift from Romanticism to Realism when he visited the pyramids. We read about him running out of water while traveling with a caravan; he suffered. Years later, he acknowledged that he'd idealized the famous prostitute Kuchuk Hanem. Was he an ethnocentrist? Because, you know, ethnocentrism was *lame*. And if he was an ethnocentrist at the beginning of his trip to Egypt, was he by the end?

We all wanted to think of ourselves as humanists, capable of releasing our cultural assumptions. But it wasn't easy to live up to our ideals.

Hilary described her experience with pushy vendors at various tourist locales. "I found myself getting really annoyed. They were mean. One pushed me really hard when I wouldn't buy a deck of cards. I realized I was getting angry, but I wasn't thinking about what it might be like to rely financially on this tourist industry. At the time I didn't stop to think what their lives might be like. I'm afraid I was ethnocentric."

Roger showed photos of a hike he took through the jungles of Vietnam. "The landscape was different from what I'm used to. I'd been in the woods, but I'd never been in the jungle. I was fascinated, but I don't know if that makes me a primitivist. I like to think that there's a universalism to appreciating nature. So, hopefully, I'm a humanist."

Most students found themselves to be a combination of two, or all three, categories. The gist of the most common analysis went something like this: "I want to be a humanist, but I know I'm an ethnocentrist. I think if I'd had more time I would have been more of a humanist. You can't let go of your own culture's assumptions in just a few days."

But a few days and good intentions were all we had.

In Cambodia, I walked through the rooms of the Tuol Sleng Genocide Museum, examining rusty tools of torture and watching Semester at Sea students cross the line into despair. At the National Museum, I talked to two monks, using sign language, for what seemed like an hour. I watched the sun set over the Mekong River.

I did not want to go back to the ship. I wanted to hop a rickshaw to the bus station and watch the nation spread out in front of me. I wanted this to be the beginning.

But as soon as it starts, it's over.

The door shuts with a soft click behind you. Crack open another book.

Between ports, Kate and I developed a new, and secret, habit: we hid out in my cabin and watched episodes of the TV series *Lost* on DVD.

"I have fifty-five papers to grade," I'd say.

"I was going to read about Turkey," she'd say.

Then we'd be in my cabin, leaning against pillows, with her computer in our laps, hunched toward the speakers, deliriously happy to be doing nothing.

"Should we watch another one?"

"I really think we should watch another one."

It was rare that we had time for more than one episode. When we did, it was inevitable that Edwin, my cabin steward, would knock on my door during his afternoon rounds.

"Hi, Edwin!" I would call. "We're busy!"

But those doors were bomb-shelter thick. Without fail, Edwin swiped his card and opened my door, then looked at us apologetically, as if he had no idea we were in there. I'm pretty sure he always knew we were in there. But he had a job to do.

"Sorry, Edwin. Don't worry about turning down the bed," I'd say.

Edwin and I developed a new routine: turning down the bed was optional. All I wanted was ice in the ice bucket. The water from the tap tasted of salt and chemicals; the ice was made from filtered water, and I filled my Nalgene with ice every afternoon and waited for it to melt. Still, despite our agreement, Edwin managed to sneak in there most days and leave my bedcover without a crinkle.

On the rare afternoon when I returned to my cabin to find the bed unmade, I felt disappointed.

Only a tiny bit.

Edwin always filled my ice bucket to the lid.

Sometimes, in the classroom, the magical moment occurs without warning: the teacher-mask falls away like sloughed skin, the hierarchy vanishes, grades become irrelevant, and suddenly it's just a bunch of people sitting in a room talking about things about which they are genuinely, personally passionate.

This happened the day we returned from Vietnam and Cambodia. The syllabus stated that we were to devote this class to the short stories of Tim O'Brien. But our minds were on the next thing, which was Burma.

"Do you guys even know anything about Burma?" I asked. My own knowledge of Burma was fresh. I'd done some reading, such as the history section of *The Lonely Planet: Myanmar*, and Mark Jenkins's "The Ghost Road," a disturbing essay about Jenkins's attempt to dodge travel restrictions and traverse an old military road in northern Burma, which was off limits to foreigners. In the most horrifying scene, Jenkins describes the first time he was stopped by Burmese authorities on the forbidden road. He was taken into a room where an official interrogated him, but both of them knew Jenkins couldn't be hurt; he was an American. Instead, the official brought in a Burmese boy, clearly enslaved by the military, and began to beat the boy, as if to say to Jenkins, *I can't touch you, but now you have to live with the fact that your actions have led to this.*

Here is a recap of the dream I had the night I read that essay. Semester at Sea was sponsoring a trip to see a Burmese man get beaten to death. I was supposed to lead the trip but I was late. When I arrived at the site, a naked man was tied down on a rack on the floor, and Burmese tour guides in military attire were throwing buckets of blood and feces on Semester at Sea students and teachers.

"This is to prepare you so you won't get sick," they said. Then they began breaking the man's ribs one by one with a hammer.

This should have tipped me off that, subconsciously, I knew there was something questionable about our going to Burma, a nation many human rights activists called on others to boycott. In my dream, SAS had sponsored this beating-to-death—paid money to make it happen—because we were curious to see something "authentic." The nature of the sponsorship rendered it instantly *inauthentic*. The drive to experience authentic "color" led to the dehumanization of a human being. It was the most dangerous form of exoticism.

Of course, it was only a dream.

"We don't know *anything* about Myanmar/Burma," several students said at once.

I told them about the military dictatorship that ruled by terror. Unlike the government in, say, Cuba, the junta did not even pretend to have any idealistic political goals to support their rule of oppression, other than the maintenance of their own power. Tourist sites, such as the Shwedagon Pagoda, had been restored for tourism by forced labor. The government shut the country off from the world. (They'd also "reclaimed" Myanmar—the country's name before the British named it Burma—making the simplest discussion of the place controversial. Was calling it Burma supporting imperialism? Was calling it Myanmar bowing to the junta?)

The human rights activists who considered it unethical to visit Burma argued that tourist money only supported the junta. One of these activists was Aung San Suu Kyi, leader of Burma's National League for Democracy. In 1991 Aung San Suu Kyi was awarded the Nobel Peace Prize for her nonviolent resistance against the military dictatorship. Now she lived under house arrest in Rangoon (Yangon).

Another such activist was Archbishop Desmond Tutu, who was slotted to sail with Semester at Sea for the Spring '07 voyage.

Gusty raised her hand. "I'm ROTC, and when I told my lieutenant I was going to Myanmar, he tried to get me to not go on Semester at Sea at all."

"Should we be going there?" I asked. Honestly, I wasn't sure we should be going to Burma. Which is not to say that I didn't really, really, really want to go to Burma. It was one of the most Buddhist countries in the world, and it had that untouched quality that reeled in the curious traveler. It was easier to meet people in a place that hadn't been jaded by tourism. Burma had a forbidden element, like Cuba. The architecture was dreamy and drippy and glittering; everything in the pictures I'd seen seemed to be made of solid gold. It was unlike anywhere I'd ever been, which made it just plain exotic.

There were good arguments for traveling to Burma. An international presence reduced the number of human rights violations. Dollars weren't that hard to get into the hands of people directly; it was all in figuring out how to do it (hiring a private truck to take you to Bago, for example, rather than taking a government bus). We could take what we'd learned and bring awareness of Burma to the States. The people, by and large, wanted us there, and we were exposing them to an alternative model of life.

We spent most of the class discussing ways we could get our money to the people, rather than the government. The books would be on the ship when we got back. The world wasn't waiting for us.

In Burma, I visited the Shwedagon Pagoda, the elaborate, gold-glittering Buddhist temple, in bare feet. I drank tea in tea stalls and swatted flies off Chinese pastries before I ate them. I asked cab drivers whether they preferred the name Burma or Myanmar; the consensus was Burma, which is the reason I have decided to call it Burma. I bought a mala, a string of glass red beads, from a monk, feeling happy to place my dollar into his hand. At the end, I hid out in a fancy hotel that Brian had booked without telling us it was fancy. And I liked it. The money we spent on the hotel went to the junta, not the people.

Of my thirty-five Exoticism students, only three felt we shouldn't have gone. They came back wearing *longis* and woven shoulder bags. They came back with stories to tell people back home.

A few months later, toward the end of the Spring '07 voyage, I received a group e-mail from a fellow Semester at Sea faculty member. Presumably because of Desmond Tutu's influence, students on the spring voyage—who'd had no contact with Burma themselves—had organized and threatened to boycott the alumni drive if Semester at Sea continued to go to Burma.

Burma was indefinitely eliminated from future voyages.

In India I signed up for a Semester at Sea organized overnight stay in a Dalit, or "untouchables," village. We spent the day at a nursing school for young Dalit women. We watched skits about a woman's ability to support herself, even if her husband died in a horrible car accident, and about the importance of education. We played catch-ball. Or perhaps it was called throwball. We heard stories about the caste system and the poverty and discrimination the Dalit people faced in the workplace, and learned some alarming statistics about the rape of Dalit women.

We slept on a roof in a Dalit village called Nalloor. Henry, our guide, joined us on the concrete roof where we would sleep, and instructed us to sit in a circle. He passed out little gold oil lamps that looked like cymbals and a woman walked the circle and filled each one with oil. Another woman came around and lit the floating wicks.

Henry spoke. "I am so grateful that Semester at Sea can spread the message of the injustice done to the Dalit people in India. You will take our message to so many people in your world. God bless you all. Let us take a moment to meditate on peace and freedom for all people."

I peeked. Everyone had their eyes closed—the quick-witted librarian, the girl in my creative writing class who rarely spoke. I closed my eyes again, and meditated on peace and freedom.

When the moment was over, Henry asked if anyone would like to sing a song. Rhonda, a student from Alabama whose father was a minister, sang a song about Jesus. Then a student I didn't know, a plain girl with wide-set eyes and a bowl cut, announced: "I'm thinking of a different song." In a low voice, she began to sing "We Shall Overcome."

Then we were all singing. And I had tears in my eyes.

There I was, free of cynicism, academic imperative, or judgment of any kind. I felt gratitude and hope. I felt good.

I signed up for a three-day tour to Cairo. Flaubert had written about his first sight of the pyramids—it seemed like the floor of his soul had just dropped out. I watched the sun rise over the pyramids. I knew how Flaubert felt.

Then I got back on the bus.

When Semester at Sea nostalgia hits, it's not about, say, India—though I feel another kind of yearning when I think of India. I wasn't done with India. Someday, I would go back, and I'd begin somewhere other than the sooty chaos of Chennai. I'd gotten short changed in Hawaii with that "cultural" center. I would have to go back. But these site-specific feelings were about the future—more hope for what I would do than memories of what I had done.

When I feel nostalgia, it's for my cabin.

At home, months later, I open the kitchen cupboard and I am hit by the strong smell of sweet Turkish coffee with its cardamom kick. This coffee, in its yellow paper sack with red Arabic writing running up the sides, is the smell of my private little square of the ship. One whiff and I'm back in my cabin with Kate, zipping up my black silk dress from Vietnam, getting ready for a social in the faculty/staff lounge, smearing sticky Egyptian sandalwood oil on the insides of my wrists with a plastic wand. There are ice cubes melting slowly in my ice bucket. My books, including newly read guides on Turkey and Croatia, are upright and aligned, because Edwin has made them so. There is the reassuring sensation of the air-conditioning. And the ceaseless rush of water past my porthole.

I forgot there were windows in Classroom 3. I got used to them.

I returned to Emerson College, where I taught the Exoticism course anew. This year, it was a kinder, gentler Exoticism.

"Flaubert is such an ethnocentrist," students would say. "He just lived in his own little bubble."

I would tell them, "Maybe we should give Flaubert a break."

HOW TO BE A TOURIST
(Cambodia)

omething about Cambodia had wormed its way inside me years before I went. There was no reason I should have zeroed in on Cambodia in particular instead of Somalia or Argentina or Lebanon. But I know it had something to do with the writer/actor Spalding Gray, on whom I developed a sizable writer-crush, and the films *Swimming to Cambodia* and *The Killing Fields*.

In my lower Manhattan neighborhood, back when I lived in New York, the Blockbuster video store carried a quirky variety of independent films. This was back when people cruised the aisles of video stores as a default evening activity, and eventually I saw a lot of films just because they were on the shelves. I must have picked up *Swimming to Cambodia* and read on the back of the box that Laurie Anderson composed and performed the soundtrack; Cambodia was not on my radar.

In this film, Spalding Gray sits at a desk and talks. He talks about his role in the Roland Joffé film *The Killing Fields* as the US consul to Cambodia during the Khmer Rouge takeover, and he talks about the time he spent in Thailand shooting the film, and he talks about the Cambodian autogenocide, and he talks about his anxious need to have a Perfect Moment when he's abroad. I mean, *he just sits there talking*. And somehow I was glued to the screen. I immediately went out and rented *The Killing Fields*, a harrowing narrative following Cambodian journalist and translator Dith Pran through Khmer Rouge hell, and left off my double feature with a nagging, low-level urge to get a firsthand sighting of this place. The sense that the nation of Cambodia was somehow potentially important to me surged up periodically over the next decade. But when your area of expertise is Latin America and your foreign language is Spanish, jobs in Cambodia are difficult to hustle up.

So when the Semester at Sea literature arrived in my mailbox several months prior to the voyage, a spark went off when I saw that it offered a trip to Cambodia. Did I care that the cost of the two-day trip was 10 percent of my Semester at Sea salary? I did not. I mailed my check so fast the envelope was likely half licked. Semester at Sea had a strict policy that international borders could not be crossed when the ship was in port; Cambodia was the only exception. When we docked in Vietnam, those of us signed up for the Cambodia trip were shuttled off to the airport and flown into Phnom Penh. Everyone else was required to remain in Vietnam.

Now here I was, in the Sunway Hotel in Phnom Penh, with a quicksand feeling at my core and a sparkling fruit juice cocktail in my hand. Fifty-seven other Americans loitered with me in the gilt-glowing lobby. Two tour buses idled outside, waiting for us to ditch our luggage so they could start moving us as fast as possible from one site to the next. A Destination Asia tour guide stood at the check-in counter making things work efficiently and without hassle; I would never ask her name and she would never offer it, though she would accompany us, always wearing a professional smile, through all major transitions for the next forty-eight hours.

After traveling in three of Semester at Sea's ports with no agenda, being in Cambodia on a packaged tour, and with this itinerary that jammed weeks' worth of activities into two days, felt all wrong. Kate and Brian, my primary travel companions, were on an independent adventure in Vietnam. They were probably riding on the backs of mopeds, slurping noodles in noisy markets, getting lost, and sleeping under thatched roofs.

But I was finally here, in Cambodia, and I was determined to make the most of it. I had to get on board if I was going to enjoy myself. Could I do this—embrace my inner Tourist with a full-body hug? Could I be the cork that bobbed along the surface of the Destination Asia tide that carried me?

Consolation #1: You know what minimizes a sinking Tourist feeling when you're in Cambodia? Air-conditioning.

Consolation #2: Most of the other fifty-seven Americans on this trip were more acquaintances than friends, but I was accompanied by one of my very best friends. In fact, for the purpose of this piece of writing, I'd call it my love interest. I'm talking about my Nikon D200. It was a beautiful machine, one I'd acquired when I learned I'd be going around the world, and I spent a lot of time just staring at it, fingering its dials, marveling at the rich-colored images it made on the screen.

What better way to embrace being a tourist than to carry a heavy, flashy camera with an unfeeling eye? If nothing else, after two days in Cambodia, I planned to have a stunning visual record.

Certainly, I suspected that being excessively focused on photography made me a potentially less ethical traveler.

Living life through a lens, especially in a new, exotic locale, it was hard to keep from seeing people as photo ops. Often, instead of trying to fit in, as with conversation, I was separating myself from the people I photographed—stepping away in order to fit them into a frame. Capturing and owning pieces of them. Diane Arbus could make all the excuses she wanted about feeling like a freak herself when she made a career out of photographing freaks. But in the end, she was putting the tattooed man and the triplets and the dwarves on display for their freakishness. There wasn't much difference in putting people, or even places, on display for their exoticness—it was all about showing that I, the photographer, had access to something off the standard grid, something compelling for its difference.

The critic Susan Sontag made a case for all photographers being "supertourists," colonizing the people and places they transformed into motionless, flat images. I didn't disagree.

So now I had to confront the possibility that with the camera in my hand, I was the ultimate tourist.

Oh, well. What could I do?

I could not think about it for a while and just take pictures. As someone who trafficked in language and ideas, it was a joy to turn down the volume on language and experience the beauty of what the eye could behold, frame, transform, expose. That's what I could do: turn on that joy.

Friday
1. Settle In

There was enough time after check-in before the first bus left to squeeze in a brief walk. Sally and I wandered into the park across the street from the hotel, where six or seven monkeys sparred on the walking path. Sally was a lovely anthropology professor from Colorado and my roommate for two nights. She carried a point-and-shoot, a Sony Super Steady Shot with a 2.5-inch LCD and 12x optical zoom. After we realized the monkeys—who seemed to be engaged in a simian variety of gang fight—would not serve as a happy memory of Cambodia, we lowered our cameras, and soon Sally spotted a family perched on a nearby bench.

"I want to take a picture of that family," Sally said.

I was apprehensive. I didn't even know how to say hello in Khmer. But before I could voice my hesitation, Sally was snapping pix of the family, and they were instantly animated. Literally, the camera brought them to life: they had been still, and now they were moving. I lifted my camera, their delight my permission. There was a shy mom with a big-headed baby in her lap, flanked by a boy and a girl somewhere between the ages of four and six. The boy and girl leapt back and forth between the bench, where they posed, and our cameras, where they marveled at the sight of themselves on the LCD screen.

The boy neared me, filling my frame with his face. He wore a bowl cut and flashed white baby teeth, a tiny half-moon of decay cutting into his left front tooth. He flirted in the direction of the lens, a perfect ham. When he ran to my side to peer into the screen, he grabbed my wrist as a hand-hold; his touch felt familiar. His mother watched with shy amusement. Even the baby with the big head looked on with intrigue.

"This one's my favorite!" Sally said, tilting her camera to show me a picture of myself in her LCD, showing the kids pictures of themselves in my LCD.

What a perfect introduction to Cambodia! Never mind what Sontag said. The camera was the key to connection, the *antitourist* device. My reluctance had almost made me walk by the bench, but the camera had brought us together. I bade good-bye to my new friends, smugly clicked the lens cap over the massive glass eye, and strolled past the entrance to Wat Penh, the most famous shrine in Cambodia, without noticing it on my way to catch the bus. My mind was on getting a good seat near the front.

2. *The National Museum*

I'd read that the Cambodian National Museum was the world's largest bat colony in an artificial structure. I once spent three days in a maze of underground caves in Tennessee where bats hibernated on the sides of the mud walls. I got as close to the bats as I could without waking them up with the heat of my headlamp; they were like mice with folded-up wings. I liked the contradiction in something so adorable that inspired universal fear.

But the bats were gone; they'd been evacuated from the museum. It turned out they'd been defecating on the art. A false ceiling had been built in 1930 to protect the art from droppings, but the job became too big. In 2003 they ushered them out and sent in battalions of do-gooders to scour bat feces off priceless artifacts.

I was disappointed by the lack of bats, additionally so because it turned out I was not galvanized by the art. Pre-Angkor, Angkor, post-Angkor, copper, bronze, Durga, Shiva, sandstone, ceramics, ethnographic objects . . . I wandered in the dark, dank interior, admiring the edgeless stone sculptures to the degree that I was able, and exited into the afternoon light.

What impressed me more than the art was the architecture of the museum. The spires on the roof were bent red roots reaching for sun. The roof was tiered, stacked sideways. It was very "Southest Asia," this building; violent and delicate, harmonious. Terra cotta popped against the blue sky.

Soon I was shooting the roof against the sky from all angles and getting crazy colors, red-orange roof intimately contrasted with impossibly blue sky, textures as solid as Cezanne paintings. Yes— that's it—the photographs were *painterly*! I was getting somewhere.

The heft of this object, the black body, the button for the finger, the window for the eye, the lens that wanted my hand. Semester at Sea students trailed in and out of the museum, taking in treasured objects. But I was here with my love object, and at the moment it was more powerful than Shiva.

Love creates an awfully shallow depth of field.

Across the street from the museum, students gathered with a k of children, some shoed and some shoeless. I placed them center of my viewfinder, but the Americans, with their shiny blond hair and nylon backpacks, kind of ruined the shot. I noticed some of the Americans reach into their backpacks and hand out whatever pens they'd brought with them, and I prickled. I knew some people considered doling out pens the solution to wanting to give something to people who asked for money, but to me it reinforced an ugly tourism dynamic. The sight of a foreigner set off a grabby air among the kids, and the foreigners, handing out something of such little value to them, feel all proud of themselves for their generosity.

Three naked boys ran nearby in the sand. That was a sight I liked better. I lifted my camera. This was when I made my first questionable decision as a traveling photographer in Cambodia.

Because, for some reason, it didn't stop me when I centered my focus on one of the boys—he must have been four—and he saw me and ran the other way.

I actually followed him, and the boys in his little gang, and I actually kept taking pictures.

I'm not saying he was scared of me. His run was playful, unhurried. I'm saying he was letting me know he didn't want his picture taken. But I thought if he let me get close enough he would change his mind. Hadn't my photographer's charm worked on the kids on the bench? Hey, I was good with kids! I could win this little guy over.

These boys were beautiful, black haired and copper skinned and sullen and wired with the energy of childhood, and they ran on honey-colored sand. The part of my brain that *saw* took over. The colors were too compelling, the way they now sat in the sand, where I'd ⸻ ı and they stopped running and sat, a perfect ⸻ ticks through the sand. . . . I couldn't let the

"*Awkun*," I tried. I waved, and I offered the back of ⸻ ⸻ oys to see themselves. They were not interested.

Later, I showed my friend Patrick, the ship photographer, the best shot. The three boys in their perfect triangle, one squatting and digging a hole with a stick, one running his fingers through the sand with his back to me, and the first boy, the only one who'd made eye contact with me, looking up forlornly with his legs outstretched. Patrick would have to admire the composition, the colors, my eye!

Patrick paused and regarded the photograph, then said, "Yeah. Pictures of naked kids are generally not a good idea."

I knew he was right. I had known it before I took those shots, but I took them anyway. And though I was not without guilt over that fact, I still thought I'd taken a good picture. Perhaps part of what I enjoyed was the direct gaze of the boy, his acknowledgment of his inability to escape from me, and the little stab of guilt I felt every time I looked at it.

3. Sunset Tour on the Mekong River

You can't take a picture of a sunset. Sunsets are clichés; photography has made them so. I tucked my camera into my messenger bag and slung the bag over my shoulder so I could use both hands for support as I boarded the rickety boat.

Our seats were unsecured plastic chairs arranged in a circle. I appreciated the unstable floor of the boat after the solid marble of the hotel. A man washed his shirt in the brown water a few feet from our dock. My friend Dwight grabbed my elbow.

"Look, Alden!" Dwight stage-whispered. "Photo op!" Dwight, a Canon man, wore his camera proudly around his neck. He pointed to the man, bare chested and chest deep with his shirt ballooning on the water in front of him. It wasn't a compelling image to me, so I left the scene to Dwight.

The boat moved up the river and soon the city we'd stood in transformed into a skyline. I flashed back to scenes from *Apocalypse*

Now, the rickety boat those doomed souls took up the river from Vietnam into Cambodia. Was this the same river?

I had not glanced at one map of Cambodia since I watched Spalding Gray unfurl one in *Swimming to Cambodia*.

It was a lucky night. The sky was streaked with shades of orange and purple thickening by the minute. Was it the curving, pointed architecture that elevated this cityscape sunset from cliché? Maybe it was still a cliché but I could see past it because it was that gorgeous. I supposed I ought to take some photographs. The light changed quickly, marking each photograph with its own distinct color palette. After some time I was able to let the camera dangle and behold the sky with my bare eyes.

By nightfall, we were shuttled from the boat to the bus to a "riverside restaurant," where we gorged ourselves at a buffet with enough food for a group three times our size. What happened to the surplus? Oh, the waste. I closed my eyes. I closed my eyes and ate.

Full bellies, memory cards fattening with image data, deep sleep to the hum of the air-conditioning in our luxury hotel.

Saturday
1. *Breakfast at Hotel*

Another buffet. Tour companies loved the buffet. Everyone was happy at a buffet. The Sunway Hotel spread featured trays of sugared donuts, bowls of cut pineapple, enormous split melons, fruit sculptures not meant to be eaten, vats of coffee, hundreds of thousands of calories, squeaky clean plates, men to whisk off and replace empty egg-bins, steam rising from mysterious meats.

I carried my plate to a table where students were discussing the fact that everyone on the program was having sex with each other.

"Surely not *everyone*," I insisted.

A student from Stanford looked down at her eggs like they were stupid.

It's not as if the faculty and staff members weren't having our little intrigues. I privately enjoyed a memory of making out with Kate on the steps of a plaza in Hong Kong. What was she up to at this moment? I bet she and Brian had booked a hut somewhere, slept in beds with mosquito nets, and woken with a vague notion of the way their day would go. I missed waking up next to Kate.

Today our tour activities were focused on Cambodia's auto-genocide and the killing fields, those elements of Cambodian history I'd learned from Spalding Gray. Had I planned this trip as an isolated journey, I might have brushed up on my history or at least watched *The Killing Fields* again before I left; but the truth was, I had whiplash from being in Hawaii and Japan and Hong Kong and Vietnam all within the past two weeks, and reading anything beyond the texts I was teaching seemed impossible. So, after breakfast I stopped in at the hotel gift shop to purchase the slim *Insight Compact Guide to Cambodia*. I speed-read it on the bus on the way to the genocide museum, slowing down when I reached the section on the Khmer Rouge and Pol Pot. Professor Moore, the history professor with whom I shared a bench seat, glanced over my shoulder, but a nod indicated to me that *he* already knew all about it.

"I'll be telling you about the Tuol Sleng Muesum as we approach our destination," our cultural tour guide, Hem, said, and then replaced the microphone on its hook.

I really liked Hem. His knowledge of his home country was encyclopedic. He came off as friendly; he smiled at the appropriate cues and was quick to answer questions with enthusiasm. But he seemed sad to me. This might have been my perception, because Hem looked to be about forty, which would have made him ten during the Khmer Rouge rampage. In any case, he was somehow exempted from the fake professional smiles sported by the nameless female tour guide, and seemed to lack fakeness in general.

Later I would ask him, "Did you lose family to the Khmer Rouge?" He would answer, "Yes. Many relatives. My father." When I looked at him, distantly stricken, he'd almost shrug, as if to say, I'm sorry, you are surprised?

Past the grime of my window I watched an alien world pass by on mute. A man on a bicycle in a thin button-down shirt and worn blue slacks kept pace next to us, then slid past the back windows and out of sight. We pushed through the low-level brown-gray haze, the smog and dust of a city, in our climate-controlled capsule.

What was so specifically horrifying about Pol Pot and the Khmer Rouge? Part of it was the fact that it was so recent. But it was also the idea of *autogenocide*, a word that didn't even exist in the Oxford English or Merriam-Webster dictionaries. Under the Khmer Rouge, children were given rifles and the authority to discern which side you were on, the new guard with their communist tenets, or the old guard, including anyone who might possibly have a reason to argue against communist tenets. If they deemed you the enemy, they had license to murder you. Pol Pot targeted ethnic Thai, Vietnamese, Buddhist monks, and other "Others," but he just as vehemently went after ethnic Cambodians to whom he had no religious objections, and the death toll of Cambodians at the hands of Cambodians was astounding.

Hem explained, "Pol Pot became dictator and the communists stormed through the country, killing everyone whom they suspected was against them, or had money and privilege, or any ties with the former government. The Khmer Rouge tortured and killed between one and two million of their own countrymen. They targeted intellectuals, teachers, doctors, and their children. They didn't just kill adults. First we will visit Tuol Sleng, one of the main detainment and torture sites."

I wasn't sure how to frame this.

2. *Tuol Sleng Museum*

The Tuol Sleng Museum, formerly a school, was a sand-colored building set back from the street and surrounded by a spiked fence the beggars outside wouldn't dare scale. Barbed wire shuttered the paneless windows at random. The former classrooms were bare, save cots and rusty metal tools of torture. Everything was the color of dry earth and rust. I nodded to students I passed as we wandered through the outdoor corridors; most gazes were glued to the cement floor.

At the Tuol Sleng Museum we moved through the communal fog of doom.

In a way, this museum preserved history as a photograph does. It was evidence that this piece of history once existed; it was proof, and in the case of the architecture and the items it held, the proof was tangible. I could reach over and feel the prickly rust on a wrench used to beat and torture people, the pinching bedsprings where torture victims were fettered. Photography with the intent to preserve this history seemed redundant; the only thing a photograph from Tuol Sleng proved was the fact that I was there.

I took a lot of photographs at Tuol Sleng.

This was the post from which they hanged the teachers from the school.

This was where they applied pliers to the nipples of uncooperative women.

Here was the wall covered by hundreds of portraits of men and women killed. Black and white. Documentary. Faces flattened by blows, expressions beaten into blankness. These shots were taken by Khmer soldiers to document Cambodia's passage to an agricultural utopia and better times. This was *their* proof.

I took photographs of the photographs. The image was the same, but the message was altered because of the photographer. I wanted these images to be a form of protest, but where would I place them to make them so?

The museum organizers had tacked hundreds of these photos next to each other. Their message was about volume, the shock value of how many faces were alive and then dead within the walls of this school. This message was more powerful than any I might have made, and the photographs I took would eventually appear only as thumbnails in my iPhoto library.

Outside, two young monks stared at the ground beside a plaque that listed the prison rules. I read the English translation:

The Security of Regulation

1. You must answer accordingly to my question—Don't turn them away.
2. Don't try to hide the facts by making pretexts this and that.
3. Don't be a fool for you are a chap who dare to thwart the revolution.
4. You must immediately answer my questions without wasting time to reflect.
5. Don't tell me either about your immoralities or the essence of the revolution.
6. While getting lashes or electrification you must not cry at all.
7. Do nothing, sit still and wait for my orders. If there is no order, keep quiet. When I ask you to do something, you must do it right away without protesting.

8. Don't make pretext about Kampuchea Krom in order to hide your secret or traitor.
9. if you don't follow all the above rules, you shall get many many lashes of electric wire.
10. if you disobey any point of my regulations you shall get either ten lashes or five shocks of electric discharge.

The monks wore eye-grabbing robes of tangerine and deep red. I held the vague notion that monks should be left alone; they were occupied with being holy. I certainly didn't want to objectify them or disturb their focus by taking their picture, so I moved toward the gift shop at the exit, where I examined dusty copies of nonbootlegged videocassettes of *The Killing Fields* and books about the genocide while sneaking peeks across the courtyard at the monks, whose calm and unreadable expressions were the source of a curiosity that would continue to grow in me, especially when, a few days later, I would find myself in Burma.

Beggars waited beyond the gate. They placed themselves between the exit and the tour buses and aggressively offered tourists their upturned hands. One man in particular hurt my heart. A missing leg presumably had been blown off by a landmine. He was skinny, bearded, and gray with dirt, and one eye appeared to be dead. He pressed closer and closer to me, leaning in on his crutch, until Hem interfered, positioning himself between the man and the bus door and me.

"Poverty," Hem said, with an apologetic half-smile.

Tuol Sleng was then. The one-legged man was the *now* that resulted from that *then*. We were catastrophe tourists, and while photographs of the still, inanimate past were possible, I c' ' ¬⁰ᵗ imagine the ability to turn my camera on the living fac suffering of now.

3. The Killing Fields

A small stupa at Choeung Ek housed skulls atop skulls atop skulls, rows of skulls taken from the body dumps, skulls with holes where bullets had passed, skulls missing jaws. All these bones had been taken from shallow pits on the grounds and assembled as a sculpture meant to scare you, the tourist. It was impossible to take in these skeleton parts, the sheer volume of them, without feeling some variation of horror.

Choeung Ek was only one of many sights like this. It was Dith Pran, the inspiration for *The Killing Fields*, who coined the term *killing fields*. The communal graves where victims of the Khmer Rouge were thrown, tossed, rolled, or otherwise unceremoniously unburied were now shallow basins lined with grass. With the soft green cover, the graves look harmless, even cozy. Many broken bodies once fit inside these dips.

Sarah, the student from Stanford, approached me holding a small spiral notebook and a pen, taking notes as she walked.

"It's amazing that most Americans don't know about these things," Sarah said. Her blue eyes, round and protruding, lent her a perpetually engaged look. "It wasn't even that long ago. You must have been alive when it was going on. Did you know?"

I nodded. "It helped that there was a movie about it," I admitted. "John Malkovich was in it."

If you've seen photographs of this site, you've seen the best photograph I took. It's the one everyone takes: a close-up of the bone pile, some skulls facing toward you, some askew.

What if I showed you this photograph, skulls filling the frame, without any context? Would it inspire horror, historical curiosity, morbid interest?

"Why did you *take* that?" one friend later asked when I showed her. Some believed photography should preserve only life's happy moments, perhaps especially the shots you take while touring. Tourism was supposed to be *fun*.

4. *The Russian Market*

Andrew was one of my party-kid students (alcohol and Vicoden was his favorite cocktail, he confessed to me at one point) who lifted weights most afternoons and always greeted me jovially. On the bus, as we pulled away from the killing fields, he cried into his hands. Two girls from Hawaii scribbled in their journals in the seat behind me.

Others were looking down at their itineraries for the next thing, asking, "What's the Russian Market?" Shopping seemed awfully frivolous after the history lessons of Tuol Sleng and Choeung Ek, but shopping occupied the next slot.

The bus doors opened to a market entrance where we confronted a surreal, color-strewn, chaotic maze of massive bargains.

"One hour," Hem said sternly, pointing his index finger to the sky. His statement was a signal shot from a gun. We had been in Vietnam a few hours ago, and we already knew what this drug felt like. For me, it was a drug that absorbed at a slower rate than it did for the students who swarmed into the aisles in the direction of bootlegged DVDs, but as I made my way into the crowded market aisles, my eyes did their dilating, and some delightful new element flowed in my bloodstream, filling me with energy.

I bought.

I bought: a lacquered box, dark wood, elaborately hand painted with red and gold design ($8); three too-small T-shirts, which I would later regret buying, including one that translated the phonetics of the Khmer alphabet, as if I would someday learn Khmer ($3); a set of six hand-sewn satin elephant Christmas ornaments ($1); a fabulous black spaghetti-strap shirt with a spare constellation of black sequins, which would become my fall-back dress-up shirt for the next three months ($3); and two overpriced silver bracelets—or maybe they weren't overpriced, but I spent too much money on them, and I considered lying, when asked, about how much they cost ($42).

Students emerged carrying soggy cardboard boxes filled with bootlegged DVDs of American movies and the TV series *Lost*, silk dresses, and faux-antique wooden statues.

Everyone was in a great mood when we got back on the bus.

I experienced a nostalgic moment at lunch (Sorya Restaurant, one hour) while we swiveled the lazy susan to spoon rice and fish from platters to plates and sipped at cold Cokes. I held my can of Coke, admiring the thickness of the frost, numb with satisfaction, thinking, *There are times I would have killed for a cold can of Coke.* This made me think of my time in Bolivia. I shared the story of my love affair with Coke in Bolivia with the students at my table.

"Similar to then, I feel like a jerk drinking Coke in Cambodia," I said.

"What's wrong with Coke?" one asked.

"I don't know, don't you think we should drink the local brews when we're traveling, instead of the most American thing you can think of?"

"Coke is good," the student explained.

We may have taken different paths, these students and I, but in the end, we were all drinking Coke.

5. The Silver Pagoda and Royal Palace

At the Royal Palace, I got to have my Perfect Moment.

In *Swimming to Cambodia*, Spalding Gray explained that he couldn't leave Thailand (despite the objections of his pissed-off girlfriend, who wanted him home) until he'd had his Perfect Moment.

He expected to have Perfect Moments in "exotic" countries, and it clearly became a source of anxiety when he didn't have them. The thing about Perfect Moments was you just didn't know when they would come.

The tourists who walked near Hem received information about the Royal Palace, its building complex, the history of the kings who occupied it, its relative recent erection, the exact number of carats of the diamonds encrusted in the Buddha, and the number of solid silver tiles upon which we were not allowed to step. We removed our shoes just to shuffle to the velvet rope that separated us from so much valuable glitter.

Those of us not near Hem wandered around the complex and *saw*.

Golden spires flexed in the sun. I couldn't get enough of those spires on the roofs of important buildings. They were like a flourish, like the end of a dance; you think it is over, but the dancer's hand transforms for a half-second into something like a fluttering bird. They called attention to beauty and served no structural purpose. I liked this beauty for beauty's sake, though of course it was difficult to capture this in a photograph in a way that hadn't been done thousands of times before.

"See, this is the kind of thing that pisses me off," my student Andrew said, staring from the silver-lined floor of the gold-spackled roof of the Temple of the Emerald Buddha. "They could fix a lot of the problems in Cambodia with the millions of dollars that one emerald is worth."

Indeed, it was a pricey gem. But tourists came to gape at old-world treasures and marvel at the worth of a rare rock, and tourist dollars were a gold that regenerated.

Being a tourist was doing a service.

Then along came my Perfect Moment.

My own idea of a "perfect" moment was one in which nothing existed but your blissful experience of that moment—a Buddhist concept, minus the self-conscious realization of the moment's perfection. Gray finally got his Perfect Moment as he swam into the open water of the Gulf of Siam off the coast of Thailand. Mine came on the heels of a sudden violent cloudburst, when I was stranded under the eaves with a pair of teenaged monks.

I first spotted the monks from far away, shaved headed and youthful, descending the stairs from the Throne Hall, gliding downward with a sexless grace. I maintained the idea that monks shouldn't be bothered, shouldn't be made into exotic objects. But my desire to take their images with me trumped what I believed. I shot from far away, with my lens jutting out to 200mm, pretending I was aiming my lens at the building, not the monks. They spotted my monstrous eye instantly, and soon they were moving up the driveway toward me.

I considered running the other way. It was a fleeting consideration, but it was one I entertained.

I *meandered* the other way, looking behind my shoulder to confirm that they were still following me.

They moved fast for monks. I let them catch up near the outdoor corridor of an adjunct palace building. A guard in a small plastic chair watched with interest as they approached me. I saw that they were very young, maybe in their midteens. The eager look on the face of the forerunner told me that they had not sought me out to reproach me for taking pictures of people (monks!) without permission; instead, they were fascinated with my camera and the fact that I used it to photograph them. They wanted to see the images of themselves on the back of my screen. They stared at their miniature, digitized selves as if they couldn't trust their eyes, wearing the unbreakable smiles of people entranced.

They wanted to pose for more pictures. We were caught up together in a cloud.

What warm color unison in the cinnamon and tangerine robes against the yellow wall of the palace building! The pair smiled shyly, unsure of how to pose. The shy, younger monk covered his mouth; the older spoke to me in an endless stream of Khmer as if he expected me to understand.

"I don't speak Khmer," I tried, shrugging, smiling, shooting.

He continued to speak nonstop, and suddenly the sky fell out and soaked us with a heavy, hot rain. We ran together to the eaves, taking cover near the guard in his plastic chair.

While it rained for the next thirty minutes the three of us exchanged information through the bilingual guard. The nineteen-year-old had been in the monastery for three years. The seventeen-year-old—beautiful, with perfect skin and bashful, girlish eyes—had just arrived. He was required to stay through the year. I took more photographs, and they asked for my e-mail address.

"Tell them I can send them the pictures if they e-mail me," I said to the guard. They will never e-mail, and that would disappoint me.

What would also disappoint me, a week later, was discovering that my focus settings had been all wrong. In a majority of shots, the monks will be slightly blurry, the background offensively sharp. A pit would form in my stomach around the well of missed opportunities.

But in a lull during the rain, when the older monk finally ran out of things to say, and I had finally taken enough pictures, we stood there close together breathing in the wet air and enjoying the sound of the rain on the golden roof over our heads, life halted in the way it only can during a Perfect Moment.

6. Fly to Siem Reap. Drive Direct to Tonle Mekong Restaurant with a Cultural Dance Show. Overnight at Borei Angkor Hotel.

Bus, airplane, bus, banquet hall. Hundreds of tourists from all over the globe congregated in a room that had no discernible beginning or ending to eat food from a buffet and watch a canned cultural dance. A forest of tripods sprouted next to tables so long they had no head or foot, and it was almost impossible to get to the buffet station, miles away, without kicking out a tripod's legs. Tripod owners glared at me with annoyance as I maneuvered my way past them and out of the claustrophobic dining cavern.

Outside, at the bar, a handful of students held bottles of Tiger beer.

"That made me want to stab myself with a fork from the buffet," I said, and ordered a beer.

The party kids were eager to get the night going, even though we had a five o'clock departure to see the sun rise over Angkor Wat. By the time we arrived at the hotel, more than a few of us had a buzz on. Hem reminded us that the bus would leave promptly at 5:00 a.m. and wait for no one while Tour Guide #2 handed out room keys.

"I'm going to bed," Sally informed me. I followed her to the elevator, which opened to reveal six or seven coeds wrapped in bath towels, wearing, apparently, the smallest articles of clothing they were able to find in their duffels.

"Is there a pool?" I asked.

"There's an *awesome* pool," they said.

Before I could decide if I wanted to wear my underwear in front of fifty-seven Semester at Sea students and faculty, I wanted to peek at the pool. Behind the elevators, the courtyard opened up to a spectacular pool, a fat and endless *S* with underwater bulbs sending light beams into the gentle ripples. Students waded in the shallow end holding cocktails, and, far away at the deep end, a game of Marco Polo was being played. A bartender in a starched shirt popped an umbrella into a daiquiri glass.

Underwear it was! I went up to my room and returned in rainbow-striped American Apparel underwear and a red J. Crew tank top.

Moore sat on a barstool with a bottle of beer, still respectably in all his clothes. "They really should have told us to pack bathing suits," he said mournfully.

We drank piña coladas and beer. We got drunk. We frolicked until late into the night. Who needed sleep? We were on vacation!

Sunday
1. Sunrise Tour of Angkor Wat

Something interesting happened at Angkor Wat at sunrise.

It wasn't the sunrise itself, sadly. Sunday was a cloudy day. The minds behind Destination Asia were not the only ones to come up with the idea of beholding Angkor Wat at sunrise, and our buses were two in a line of parallel-parked tourist vehicles that let out hundreds of tourists like us. A hot air balloon drifted toward the temple, and we waited, chins in our hands, for something breathtaking to happen.

Was the main temple of Angkor Wat breathtaking? It was. Of course it was. Its grandness, the miracle that it stands, its melty stone and intricate towers and endlessly high and narrow staircases—it was a gorgeous sight. But you've seen it before. Like sunsets, photography has ruined the firsthand impact of major architectural marvels. I took a few shots, the kind that said I was there. Sally and I posed together in front of the reflecting pond with the temple in the background. It would be a good memory.

I perched on the edge of a stone stairway, trying to ascertain whether the sunrise was officially over, next to a group of young British travelers. The reflection pool in our line of view mirrored the peaks and dips of the temple, casting back a paler and paler blue.

"Was that it?" one of the Brits asked.

"That was it," we collectively agreed. The Brits picked up their packs and moved on.

Then the interesting thing happened.

I got to be the Exotic Object.

Without warning, three Asian tourists rushed over to set up tripods at the foot of the stone staircase where I sat yawning. But instead of mounting their cameras to face the temple, they oriented them toward me. Then they frantically began taking pictures. Of me.

I looked around, perplexed. Had they mistaken me for someone famous? I had once been mistaken for Jennie Garth in a Madrid train station, but that was a stretch. I didn't look like anyone famous. I felt I should smile, but I was bewildered by the motives of these photographers from afar, and wasn't sure if I should comply with their expectations. The look that they captured was *stunned*.

What did they want from me? I was just an American tourist.

More shutterbugs flocked. Soon there were a dozen, then two dozen Asians with cameras on tripods taking pictures of me; then, one by one, they climbed the stone steps, flung an arm over my shoulder without so much as a hello, and smiled for the paparazzi.

"Where are you from?" I asked the middle-aged woman with the floppy beige sun hat.

"China!" she said, but she was not interested in conversation, even via facial expressions or sign language. None of them were. Their half-hugs were intimate, but the lack of eye contact meant there was no interest in connection.

Afterward, I sat on the stone steps, feeling mugged. But also, I felt interesting. I was someone they wanted to remember; I represented something they valued. My race? My Americanness? The weird candy-apple-red-and-blond hair?

I deserved the confusion this pairing offered me.

2. Ta Prohm

But I'd never seen pictures of Ta Prohm. Strangler figs and silk cotton trees choked the temple walls. Tree roots like monster fingers reached down to grab the stone. It was as if a sourceless set of rivers froze while tumbling over the rocks and pooled on hard-packed earth that refused to absorb it. Ta Prohm was nature versus hard-won construction. Even the rubble, broken bricks of copper-colored stone, was beautiful to look at.

The light was kind. I set the white balance to "sunny" and the ISO to 100. I stepped in front of tourists as they examined the details of the walls, the small dancing figures, these miracles of miniature.

Inside the Ta Prohm complex, far away from where I stood, a group of young Cambodian dancers rested between numbers. Two were costumed in shimmery fabrics with golden headgear that mimicked the spires of the National Palace and the museum. They loitered with plain-clothed companions, young girls, perhaps waiting for tourists to request a dance.

They were there to make money. I supposed I could ask them to pose and offer them a dollar. But they were too far away, and I didn't want a posed photo; I wanted the "between the acts" shot, the one Annie Leibovitz would have taken during her *Rolling Stone* days. I extended the zoom on my lens and released the shutter.

By now I should have known that distance didn't matter; when that eye pointed at you, you looked back, you saw it.

These dancers, too, obviously knew how to spot the unwanted (unpaying) eye. There was no bewilderment or time lapse between what they saw and what they understood. What they did was look at me with anger so that that was all I got from them.

This became one of my favorite shots from my time in Cambodia. It was a record of the moment I was caught red-handed taking something from someone without offering anything in return.

Of course, at the same time, with its headgear, shimmery fabrics, and temple backdrop, it was a photograph with a lot of straight-up exotic appeal.

It told the story of my tourist guilt even better than the shot of the naked boys in the sand.

3.–7. *Leper King, Elephant Terraces, Bayon, Baphuon, South Gate of Angkor Thom*

We managed to squeeze it all in until we ran out of time just before the Elephant Terraces.

"There are the Elephant Terraces," Hem said sheepishly, pointing through the windshield of the bus as we drove past. I took a picture out the window and moved to the cooler for a cold can of Coke.

Then I was back on the plane.

Back in Ho Chi Minh City, which I stubbornly referred to as Saigon, Kate and I had our first official date.

When in port, it was virtually impossible to avoid other Semester at Sea passengers. Any hotel or restaurant listed in *Lonely Planet* or *Moon Guide* or *Fodor's* or *Let's Go* was crawling with them. But a friend in Hong Kong had given Kate and me an insider's guide to Vietnam printed in the UK, and that was how we found the secluded, romantic restaurant to have our first private meal.

The restaurant was set back from the busy street. A porch bar hid in a tangle of junglelike foliage. We ordered martinis and, moments later, asked for two more martinis, but could they make them twice as big? Vietnamese martinis were so shrimpy I was almost offended.

Kate lived in Portland, Oregon, across the country from where I lived. But she was born and raised in Massachusetts and missed her family there. Tonight she said, "I've been thinking a lot about moving back to the East Coast. Maybe Brooklyn."

I said, "What about Boston?" It seemed early for this suggestion. We had great fun together, but we had only known each other traveling, and everyone knew that traveling was not real life. But for both Kate and me, the fact that we loved traveling together was a strong indication that we were compatible in other important ways.

In the dining room, the waiter tossed rose petals atop our table. It was easy to put the Cambodian genocide behind me and become more interested in the miracle of goat cheese in a salad and staring into the eyes of the person I was starting to love. I chose not to carry a camera on this important date, recognizing that documenting it required stepping out of the moment. Which is, of course, why I used to travel without a camera, before my tour group days.

Back on the ship, I connected the USB cord from my camera to my laptop. I patiently waited through the slideshow of thumbnails as the contents of my memory card transferred.

Some details were too small to see on the small camera screen. For one, it was hard to tell when the focus was off. I relied on the intelligence of autofocus, but I still hadn't mastered the focal settings. One point. Closest point. Average from eight given points. I don't know. I "used instinct" because I was intimidated by the Nikon D200 manual, which I'd read through more than once with a sincere attempt to understand it. I mean, I was an English teacher who taught at an arts school. My right brain was a bully that had turned my left brain into a cowering little weakling.

Later I would learn that it was not just me. A fatal flaw in focal functions of the D200 model meant that many of its owners were plagued by focus problems.

Quite a few of my pictures from Cambodia were blurry.

At the desk in my cabin, watching the slide show of images, I leaned my cheek against my hand and accused myself of hubris. I should have brought a point-and-shoot. I was not worthy of that mammoth machine. Oh, some of them were good. Probably half of the photos of the teenage monks were very good. One would be sold at an auction on the ship and two would appear in a respectable magazine. I'd done a few things right. But where had I gone wrong with the majority?

There were many things I never learned in Cambodia.

Basic things—I didn't know them. I didn't know the visual difference between the Mekong River and the Mekong Delta. I did know that the French colonized Cambodia, but I didn't know how long the rule lasted, or when it ended, and I didn't know that the name of the killing fields I visited was Choeng Ek until I came home and looked it up so I could cite it in an essay I was writing about being a tourist in Cambodia on a honeymoon with a Nikon D200. I didn't know that the skulls at Choeng Ek were arranged by age and gender or why it would have been worse to look at these skulls if I had known that fact. I never learned how old Hem was, or what happened to his father, or what he'd seen as a child, because I didn't know if it was okay to ask. I didn't know the name of a single Cambodian king. I didn't know how to say a word in Khmer beyond *awkun*. And I didn't even have to use that word much, because I'd paid someone to do the thanking.

But what I took away from Cambodia, the thing that plagued me, was the fact that I didn't understand this one thing. It haunted me. It wasn't that I couldn't do it. It was that I didn't understand the difference between what I was doing when I took a picture that was blurry and what I was doing when I took a picture that was not.

Months later, just after I returned to the States, my parents took me out to dinner.

"What was your favorite country?" my mom asked.

I told them the place I couldn't get off my mind was Cambodia. "I should probably watch *The Killing Fields* again, now that I've actually been to the killing fields," I said.

"You know Dith Pran took your father's photograph for the *New York Times*," my mom said.

I looked at my dad, shocked. "*Huh?*" I said. My father was often photographed. The golf courses he designed and redesigned were the frequent sites of major golf tournaments. My grandfather, also a well-known golf course architect, was a media presence as well; he had once been photographed by Annie Leibovitz for an American Express ad. But how had my dad never mentioned being photographed by Dith Pran for the *New York Times*?

"It's true," he said. "A few years ago he came to Montclair to take my picture for a piece on Bethpage. He was an interesting guy. We spent a long time talking about his life in Cambodia. He took almost an hour getting the shot right; he was very meticulous."

The man who had inspired the film that had inspired the man who had inspired me to go to Cambodia knew my father. A connection was secured; the two of them had occupied space together, and there was a photograph to prove it. I felt a circuit had closed. For Christmas that year, my father gave me a personally inscribed copy of the book Pran edited, *Children of Cambodia's Killing Fields*.

Long after I'd traded in my Nikon D200 for a new model and eradicated my focus errors, and far beyond my fear of being the ultimate Tourist, the stories of those children haunted me.

THE BURMESE DREAMS SERIES
(Burma)

The pictures tell you I was there. I took the pictures of the cows lolling and the water buffalo lumbering in herds. I took the pictures of the novice monk with the suitcase, walking along the road, between towns, in the middle of what appeared to be nowhere. The photographs are blurred and soft; the greens are especially vibrant. I have no pictures of myself in this landscape. I was only behind, never in front of, the lens of a large and powerful camera.

I saw the countryside of Burma through the windows of a bus. I can't say the others on the bus were a friendly bunch—at least, there was little of the camaraderie one might hope to find while traveling. A short while into the bus trip, we went over an unexpected bump as I was taking a swig from my wide-mouthed water bottle. The water flew back and soaked my face, my dress—water dripped down my chin. I sputtered and looked around for someone to share the joke with, but the Canadian across the aisle from me just turned, observed, and then went back to his bus-riding stare. I was pretty much on this trip alone, though it was a group trip, another paid-for Semester at Sea package.

We were on our way to Kyaiktiyo from the capital city of Rangoon. The trip would take all morning. I was spread out across two seats—the bus was only half full—with my camera in my lap and, in the seat pocket in front of me, a bunch of miniature bananas I'd bought from a pushy girl on the street. I was going to Kyaiktiyo to see the Golden Rock, a miracle of physics and a Buddhist pilgrimage site. I'd seen pictures: a boulder like a misshapen potato dangling on the very edge of a cliff. Supposedly, a hair of the Buddha kept it balanced there. Buddhists had painted on layers of gold leaf, and a stupa, which housed the hair, was built atop.

Because I would be in Burma only a few days, I experienced a vague anxiety while staring out the window, watching the rural landscapes blow past through grimy glass. I wanted to be going to Kyaiktiyo, to see a new region of Burma, a Golden Rock, but I didn't necessarily want to be on a bus. Outside there was a world, with air: buffalo herders kicking aside reeds, rickety bridges leading to huts on stilts, men fishing with holey green nets. I saw a one-room wooden house that had lost many planks, next to which sat the longest pig I'd ever seen. In my fantasy I was out there in rubber boots and a straw hat, a few dollars' worth of kyat in my pocket, a scrap of bread in my knapsack, my camera slung around my neck. Maybe an extra memory card tucked into my front pocket. A water bottle. And something to share with the Burmese I would meet, something edible. I had heard salt was gold in Burma, but it was just something I'd heard. I would have to ascertain what was of high value to the senses in these parts, and hope it was something that would fit in my small, imaginary burlap sack.

Of course I didn't want to be on a bus. But on foot, in one morning, I would have interacted with the pig, perhaps, and one or two farmers. Tearing through the countryside like this, I watched the landscape change at breakneck speed; I saw miles in minutes. A town busy with fruit shoppers at one glance, a ramshackle village the next. Marsh, tracks but no trains, crowded bus stops, crowded trucks carrying people away from bus stops, baskets on heads and on the backs of bikes, solitary monks standing on the side of the road. The child monk swinging that mysterious suitcase.

And so I did what only an amateur would do, because this was my chance: I took pictures out the window. This would be my Burma. The blurry buffalo and soft-focus bent willows. A sign in Burmese streaked with window glare and freckled with dirt. In four hours I stopped shooting long enough to eat two mini-bananas and spill water down my dress again. The rest of the time I kneeled on the seat, my camera at the ready. Sometimes, the people outside the bus saw me, smiled from the road, or cocked their heads in curiosity.

I had my favorite interaction in Burma this way. For a few moments, our bus kept time with a truck, its height our height, with a black plastic tarp covering the goods it carried. Three young men—they could have been eighteen or thirty—had hitched a ride and were sitting on the tarp, their legs dangling over the back. This looked like a fun way to travel, out in the wind. The men wore baseball caps and thin clothes and nothing on their feet. They saw me right away. This was one of the only times I was eye level with anyone outside the bus. I lowered my camera, smiled, and waved. They smiled with their mouths open, waved back. They motioned for my camera, mimed taking a picture, so I lifted my lens and aimed it at them. Then I put my camera down and we stared at each other with wonder until the bus pulled ahead of the truck. I can't know what they were thinking, but it felt to me we had shared something akin to the mute awe of people who'd just realized they were in love. We weren't ten feet away from each other, but if they'd spoken, I wouldn't have heard them; they knew this. We all knew not to bother speaking.

The Burmese I met did not seem worried about speaking to me. I'd been told it might be dangerous for them to talk to foreigners. If they were caught telling us about the government, the nature of their oppression—the systematic rape, the burning of villages, the economic chaos, their beloved rightful leader under house arrest—they risked big trouble. We risked nothing. But still I held fear. I feared I had the power to cause big trouble just by being in Burma. But in my first hour in Rangoon, at the Shwedagon Pagoda, a monk approached me and asked if I wanted to visit his monastery. He led me into a gilded room for shade and I sat with him on the floor and he answered my questions about his life as a monk. Suddenly he said, "Listen. I can only talk to you longer if you are serious about learning about Buddhism at our monastery. If you're not serious, you understand, I need to spend my time talking to someone else." I recognized that I felt nervous; I was worried about letting him down, but also about being tricked. Perhaps it would have bettered me had I gone with him. But all reason told me not to wander off alone with a stranger in a city I didn't know, even if this stranger were a monk. I offered my regrets; the monk smiled and wished me peace. He couldn't have been more than twenty-five. This meant he had known life only under the junta; they had ruled as Big Brother for forty-six years. Still he managed to hold peace in his heart.

There is a chance I might have disrupted his peace just by changing the subject. Monks were imprisoned for marching in the streets. All they had to do was hold up a sign saying "democracy" or "freedom" and they'd get three years in jail. Monks were not off limits for legal murder. When I saw the boys on the back of the truck, I knew, because of the glass between us, that I could do them no harm.

In Kyaiktiyo, I hiked with a small group to the top of the mountain toward the Rock. It was a long, winding, mostly paved road, and the vistas were muffled by fog. We stayed in a hotel that reeked of mold; I sneezed the whole night. I felt guilty because, after I had booked the trip, I read in *Lonely Planet: Myanmar (Burma)* that this hotel was owned and run by the military junta; it was the one place Lonely Planet had singled out to avoid. As a tourist, it was hard to get your money past the strangle-holding junta. Any kyat or dollars spent probably went to them, unless you hired private transportation or bought your wares on the street. So far, I was pretty sure the only kyat I'd gotten to the people was to the pushy girl with the bananas.

In the morning we hiked the rest of the way to the Rock. It was more magnificent than it was in the pictures. It's not always this way with landmarks; I'm just as often let down. But this rock did defy gravity. There was no reason it should be there. Natural laws should have ordered it rolling down the side of the mountain. As much of a miracle, to me, was how men got the gold paint all over the rock, or built a stupa atop, without being the straw on the Rock's back, or falling off themselves and dying. Maybe men did die doing this. I got as close as I could, but only men were allowed past a certain stretch of rope. Men were touching the rock, pleading and praying. Monks wandered the courtyard asking for alms, their bowls overturned, a few kyat on top.

On the hike down, we passed pairs of monks heading toward the Rock in walking meditation. I didn't take pictures of them. I looked forward to getting back on the bus and taking pictures that way. I didn't care that the other tourists on the bus thought I was doing something fruitless and possibly immature. I illogically hoped the windows had been cleaned, but when we arrived at the bus, I saw that they were grimier. The ride, toward the end, had been a mud-splash.

Before heading back to Rangoon, we did some things that eased my mind. Our tour guide took us to a small town and led us on foot down a dirt road where a woman was weaving *longis* in her floorless wooden house. The woman did not seem to care that we were there; she kept her eyes on the loom. She pumped her feet on the pedals and braided the strings, her fingers fast as spiders' legs. *Longis* are like sarongs, Burmese wear them every day, and I might wear something like this not knowing where it had come from. But seeing it woven, watching the antiquated wooden loom move and listening to its clack, I had to buy two. The *longis* smelled like mold. I would wash them by hand so the dye wouldn't run. I knew the money went to the woman weaving. My guide deserved his cut. Afterward, while other tourists selected *longis*, I wandered to the street into a small clot of boys and young men. None spoke English, but one spoke Spanish. "How do you speak Spanish?" I asked the boy in Spanish. "Someone came here once who spoke Spanish, and he taught me." I'd spent ten years in school and two years abroad learning that language. The boy's ability baffled me. Our guide, similarly, had never been outside of Burma, and his English might have been better than mine—it was British English.

I took few pictures until I got back on the bus. Then I shot, shot, shot. A man leaning on a motorcycle in a rain-washed mud town. Miles of reeds, willows, cows, buffalo. Eventually, when I got them up on the computer screen, I saw the glass had rendered them blurrier than I'd expected. Some part of my brain had convinced me that the images would be there as I saw them, sharp.

I showed a selection to my friend Patrick, the real photographer. "Why are they blurry?" he asked. He looked longer. He frowned. "Did you take these out a bus window?"

"What if I said it was a filter?" I asked. Technically, it was.

I discovered that I liked the blur in the photographs. I liked the haze. They made the images of Burma dreamy, surreal, which is how it was to me. I liked that the filter was the tourist's shield. I could even say I'd done it on purpose: the work reflects the tourist's view of Burma. The countryside looked easy and peaceful to us. Herders and workers lived their daily lives outside our fast-moving machine.

What we saw and remembered did not reflect the true Burmese experience, lives lived suffering memories of torture, a sister raped, a son stolen. No. I saw willows.

I had the reasonable suspicion that no one liked these pictures as much as I did. They were blurry, the primary photographic flaw. My pictures were like misspelled poems. Nevertheless, I felt happy when I looked at them, and I submitted them to a few shows. One was taken by a gallery, and a Boston café offered me two walls for two months.

I hung my show at Ula Café on May 2, 2008. Kate was here now. She had moved to Boston and we had rented an apartment together. She helped me nail in the supports and hang the frames on wires. I called the series "Burmese Dreams." The monks, the buffalo, the boys on the truck. My favorite is of a child standing with his hand against a brick wall, looking up at the viewer with a curious alarm. The boy leaned on a sign that said several things in beautiful, curly Burmese, and, in the middle, in English, SHMOL IN POWER. It was a scary mystery to me, this painted scrawl: I'd glimpsed something that may have been sinister without even knowing it.

When we were done hanging, I stood back and admired the evenness of the frames with the hammer in my hand.

The girl at the register said she liked them. Then she asked, with what I took to be respect, a query regarding my artistic vision: "Why are they blurry?" I told the girl my lies, which had become the truth.

The day after I hung the show, Cyclone Nargis struck Burma from the south and blasted the Rangoon region, where my bus ride ended. I always thought cyclones belonged in the plains of my country, as in *The Wizard of Oz*. In many ways Burma is, to me, like *The Wizard of Oz*, which was Dorothy's dream. It seems like a place I've seen in a movie or read about in a book, some kind of inspired exaggeration.

If you look at the satellite maps of the day it hit, Cyclone Nargis is a lovely swirl over the country of Burma. But on the ground it was mean and brutal. It left over two million hungry and homeless, over one hundred thousand dead. A few things in particular upset me when I heard about Nargis, aside from the obvious. One was the number of children wandering alone in Rangoon looking for their families, how many had been orphaned. Then came the news that the junta was not accepting aid from certain sources, and no aid workers period. They accepted supplies. Many of those supplies they decorated with their own stamp to make the Burmese people think it was their own government's aid. I started to think about Somoza in Nicaragua after the earthquake razed the capital in 1972: He took the aid and kept it for himself. He took the blood the Red Cross gave them for the wounded, and sold it. The junta had already done worse things than that, a little genocide here and there.

But still, it was a hazy, distant kind of dread I felt about Burma post-cyclone. For two months I visited this café, which was near my home; as I walked there I meditated on the powers of espresso. I stood in line at the counter and examined baked goods. At some point I would look up, and there it was, neatly organized on the walls: my Burma. Oh, right, Burma. A land far away.

It dawned on me slowly during the first days of my show that much of what was in my pictures was not there anymore. The cyclone had wasted the landscape. Fishing rafts had been washed away. Trucks stripped of their tarps. Stilts kicked out from under houses. How many people in those pictures must be dead. Most of those people—I know they're dead.

Maybe the boys on the back of that truck still live. There are miracles, maybe. As far as I know, the Golden Rock still rests on the lip of the cliff.

I Know What You Did in Egypt

A Letter to Gustave Flaubert
(Egypt)

Dear Gustave Flaubert,

I don't know how you would feel about this, but I've read all the letters to your mother and your friend Louis that you wrote while you were in Egypt. I've also read parts of your diary.

An editor named Francis Steegmuller ransacked your files and decided it would be a good idea to take these pages and bind them together as a book. He called it *Flaubert in Egypt*. It was the book you never meant to write. I teach this as a text every year; I've read it now eight or nine times. The first time I approached it as a scholar. But after several reads I realized the thrill I got was because I knew I was snooping, and now I feel compelled to attempt some connection with you, to come clean.

I also write because my feelings toward you, reading and rereading this text, have evolved, and I've been feeling an unexpected kinship with you of late. Initially, you were a villain (and in some ways you still are), an ethnocentrist traipsing about North Africa with a grin on his face that came from all the special treatment he got as a Frenchman, a member of an oppressive class. You watched women get raped and responded with a shrug, observed men being beaten and laughed till you peed in your pants. Yes, you have what I consider to be an ugly side. But things are not as black and white as I once believed they were.

What I'm interested in is the fact that you changed. Something about being in North Africa changed you as a writer. You were an average writer before you went to Egypt and a good writer when you got back; Steegmuller even suggests that Egypt made you the man who could write *Madame Bovary*, that enduring and excellent novel. Who would have known, having read your earlier work, the drippy, hyperbolic prose and invented landscapes you'd adapted from history books, that you could write a masterpiece of quotidian French life? I heard that your friends Maxime and Louis stayed up all night with you as you read aloud what you'd written of your Saint Anthony book before you went to Egypt. They listened to you without offering any comments until you turned the last page, and then, when you were done, promptly told you to burn the manuscript—that its release would embarrass you. I know this must have been devastating. I've certainly started writing projects that went into the drawer (though nothing as long as *Saint Anthony*—yikes). And I think my drawer might contain some similar false starts. You and I both wanted to write about *elsewhere*, about places we didn't really understand. Too much can go wrong when you claim authority over something you don't know enough about. That happened to me when I tried to write a longer piece "about Cuba," and I'd been there five times. I never grasped the intricacies of that place in an ownership kind of way. Who could, except a Cuban?

When you went to Egypt with Maxime it was a more grueling journey than most of us can understand today. It wasn't like you went to complete some task that we all knew to be harrowing, as we might, today, consider climbing a 17,000-foot volcano in Mexico, wearing cramp-ons, getting snow blind, and risking frostbite. You were off on a whim when you went to Egypt, but it was far, far away.

You were older than I was when I took my first big trip—you were twenty-seven when you left, I think—and I know that it was much harder for you to leave your mother than it was for me. (I mention this because your obsession with your mother was downright unsettling, frankly . . . but I can relate to the difficulty of leaving loved ones behind for what amounts to a whim.) I could be home within a few hours if the need or desire had arisen, and there was always the phone—and still, when my mother took me to the Newark airport to see me off when I went to spend the year in Costa Rica, we clung to each other and cried. It was a surprise to learn that I was terrified. I was twenty-two. I had a backpack with fourteen books and four dresses in it. And pens and countless sheets of paper. Lined, unlined, bound, unbound. So much paper. There was no e-mail then, and phone calls were impossible; there were only letters. Letters that you wrote with a pen, on whatever paper you had at hand, for which you had to find an envelope, stamps, and a post box. I used to write and wait for letters as if they were lifelines.

This is the first real letter I've written in about a decade.

I wish I could lick the flap and know you'd tear it open with your thumb.

Your buddy Maxime spilled a lot of gossip about you after you died. The worst exposure, what your friends and family were most angry over, was that he gave away the secret of your epileptic fits, your biggest weakness, as they saw it. And Maxime said you moped. You moped when the mail came in Egypt and there was nothing in it for you. You moped when Egypt briefly lost its "charm." Well, after two years, I imagine the charm would wear off. That was the problem, wasn't it? Charm wears off if you stay still too long. And the charm of the unfamiliar is what we go so far away for in the first place.

I remember during my sixth month living in La Victoria, Costa Rica, there was this one moment when, sitting at the school where I taught, methodically eating the cookies they were selling to raise money for the school—chocolate with crème filling, chalky Oreo imitations—I looked out at the cornfield next to the highway and I almost said out loud: "In six months nothing has changed here. Nothing has changed except the kids have longer hair and the corn has grown taller." My friends all had office jobs in New York. At that moment, staring at the corn, I fantasized about desks and air-conditioning and restaurant lunches. I was no longer fulfilled by weekends staring out at the Caribbean Sea; the sight of the perfect water made me feel anxious and idle. It was normal, at that point, to wash my clothes with a big bar of blue soap and hang them on barbed wire to dry. Rotting teeth in my students' mouths were normal. Spiders the size of a first grader's hand were simply something you shook out of your towel. The excitement had worn off. But I'd made a commitment, and the joys of my life there had become about something else—the relationships I'd made, a deep appreciation for my surroundings (when I was in Cahuita having a *batido de banano en leche* while staring at the Caribbean Sea, for example, but equally when snuggled up with my student Rosa Elena, having coffee and saltines with her family in their ramshackle home). In the end it was about something much different from what it was at the outset—what I left with was far more real. Like, *real life*. Which is what I'd been trying to transcend. It wasn't until I went back to the States that I felt culture shock again—shock the first time I entered a department store and saw the sea of clothes that were unnecessarily fine; shock when I mentally added up the numbers on the price tags and thought about how far that money would go for the school where I taught. I didn't have a full-blown panic attack, but I did suddenly feel all wrong, and I had to sit down on the floor between the racks of winter wraps and coats with faux-fur collars. It wasn't necessarily a good feeling. But it was a *big* feeling.

I know all about the sexually transmitted diseases you picked up from your whoring.

I have complicated feelings about prostitution. I think it should be legalized. I feel excluded from it. I have vague distaste for men who visit prostitutes, but no umbrella moral objection, as long as those marketing their bodies are doing so by choice. I do believe there's a foul flavor of a Western man seeking prostitutes abroad, especially in poorer nations. But here's what I don't ever tell anyone: I realized recently that I am a tad jealous about your whoring lifestyle. Yes, you died from it. A cerebral hemorrhage at fifty-eight years old, complications from various sexually transmitted diseases; you made some bad choices around your sexual activity, indeed. I'm isolating the whoring you wrote about during your time in Egypt. (Whoever translated your letters, which I've been reading over lately, has gotten me using *whore* as a verb! It's simultaneously Victorian and present-day rude, not my standard way of speaking.) Your whoring in France seemed only decadent to me, from how you described it: "The next two days I lived lavishly—huge dinners, quantities of wine, whores. The senses are not far removed from the emotions, and my poor, tortured nerves needed a little relaxation." But in Egypt your double-magic male key offered you an *in* to the culture that I didn't have. You gave the famous "dancer" Kuchuk Hanem money, she invited you into her home; you were served tea, she and the other dancers laughed with

you, you could ask them questions, you bantered, it was agreed
that physical contact was free of hostility, you could actually have a
conversation, however falsely constructed to serve your needs. Believe
me, I have my issues with this, but when I wandered the streets of
Cairo, ignored by the women, harassed by the men, I wished for an
easy *in* of some kind.

When I was in Egypt I did the things one did: I watched the sun
rise over the pyramids and took a dinner cruise on the Nile. But parts
of this were distressing, especially the Nile cruise, which wound up
feeling a little like a Bar Mitzvah. The band played "Mambo #5" ("a
little bit of Tina all night long") and successfully coerced a group of
Americans into a conga line. I couldn't believe it. And the Nile itself,
the segment we traveled, was no more impressive than, say, the
Charles River in Boston. I guess I was expecting it to look as it did
when you saw it: Wild. Actual riverbanks instead of the concrete
walls containing it. Maybe a few snakes dangling from trees. Not
tacky plastic store signs. It might have been New Jersey.

My Egypt. A dam of dead horses. Sandalwood oil as tenacious as
tree sap. A hookah bar where they played "Sandstorm," the techno
song unappreciated by those who've never done Ecstasy. (Oh, dear
sensual friend, would you love Ecstasy.) A plastic sack of saffron.
A rough hand on my elbow—a strange man in the market. Falafel
seconds out of the fryer. A mad cab ride, during which my driver hit
a pedestrian and kept on going. An actual sandstorm the morning
I watched the sun rise over the pyramids: sand blowing down the
backs of my shoes, into my mouth, plastering my hands so that I
spent the day with my fingers spread apart; one finger rubbing against
another finger was like nails on a chalkboard.

It was beautiful, the sun rising over the pyramids. We early risers
stationed ourselves up on a bluff of sand. Rows of tour buses lined up

behind us. Ahead, those great wonders of the world. A depth you can't perceive in the best photographs. Cairo beyond the pyramids, in the distance, smog-blurred like Los Angeles. The sun rose like a gas flame: blue-bottomed sky, heating into oranges and yellows. The color of the sky changed by the moment, and the air warmed by the moment. I was wrapped in a plum-colored wool scarf against the cold and the wind. The Sphinx—where was it? It was so much smaller than I'd guessed. It was freezing and the air was sandpapered with desert dust, scratching my cheeks. Too often, I had to close my eyes.

When the sun was up we made our way down to the enclosure of the pyramids. A pair of thirteen-year-old American boys launched lacrosse balls back and forth in front of the Great Pyramid. Camel masters chanted at us, "Ride a camel, ride a camel." Looking back I wish I'd ridden a camel, but at the time I didn't want to endorse this tourist novelty that had arisen from a stereotype. Egypt, the land of pyramids and camels—here we are, offering you both at the same time!

Also, I didn't want my jeans to smell like camel.

There was nowhere to get coffee in or near the pyramid complex. I had gotten up at something like four in the morning; it was still too early for the stalls to be open. But of all the amenities to be unavailable—*coffee?* I walked around the grounds half-lidded. I tried to be properly awed by the whole thing, but I was having a hard time. The lacrosse sticks, the absence of caffeine in my bloodstream, the camel-pushing men, the constant demand for "baksheesh, baksheesh"—even the uniformed guards were trying to get into my pockets. I took a picture of a camel and the driver tailed me until I gave him baksheesh. And while there was no coffee for the tourists, there were theater lights fixed into the ground; every night tourists beheld a light show at the pyramids, a spectacle, a modern theatrical imposition on what was valued for its being ancient. A huge stage, scaffolding exposed, preceded the Sphinx, and folding chairs got in the way of our photographs. I tried to imagine the great Giza pyramid complex as it was when you had seen it: great wonders rising up from the sand.

You know what my favorite part of the Great Pyramid is? The "unfinished chamber." It's underground, and though Egyptologists suspect it was first intended to be King Khufu's burial chamber, no one knows for sure what it was for. I didn't even see it, and I think that's why I like it: it's a *mystery* to me. I like the *idea*.

The Sphinx was cool, too. Majestic. It stared off with stern disinterest, as if to say, "Who cares that I'm smaller than those pyramids? I know I'm awesome."

You said the Sphinx "fixed you with a terrible stare." It made you giddy and Maxime pale.

That Sphinx has personality.

Edward Saïd said that Westerners do not discover the East; they only rediscover it. It is already in our Western consciousness. We have, in fact, created the East—the reality is secondary to the idea of the place. You were a pure Orientalist that way; Saïd even quoted you in his book. (He doesn't like you.) You'd already written about what it was like to first see the pyramids before you went to Egypt. You'd barely even seen a photograph; there weren't any back then. When you finally did stand in the actual sands of the desert, you observed the scene fresh. You had to take a journey with guides on horses and drinking water and food to get there, and there were no theater lights. There were no weary camels tied up waiting for the next tourist to awkwardly scramble onto their backs. There was no admission fee and there were no ropes. There was no one there but you, nothing between you and Pyramid of Khufu, the last remaining Wonder of the Ancient World.

Maxime recounted his sighting of the Sphinx as a "confrontation of a monster." He said he had never been so moved in his life. You, apparently, reined in your horse and cried out: "I have seen the Sphinx fleeing toward Libya! It was galloping like a jackal!" And when Maxime looked at you funny, you added, "That's from *Saint Anthony.*"

Your Saint Anthony book, the one Maxime and Louis hated: Aren't you glad it was never out there? I'm going to say this only because I know you can take it: some of your pre-Bovary Romantic prose cracked me up. What you wrote about the pyramids verged on adorable. *You*, Gustave, who went down in history as a writer of bronze-y declarative sentences, ones you hammered out until they gleamed, once wrote with no restraint at all. The climber of your imagined pyramids? He arrived with fingernails torn and bleeding! Soul soaring! Ears ringing with the unimaginable magnificence of it! His entire existence flooded before him like a dream! (I'm paraphrasing, but that's really how it reads.)

O Gustave! I bet you wish your young overstated exclamations had stayed in the drawer and out of the hands of curious critics.

Don't just blame Steegmuller. Blame Maxime. Blame Graham Greene. Those "travel writers" thought your letters and journal entries should count as literature, be collected and bound and sold, even though they both knew you considered travel writing a base genre, and you wanted nothing to do with it.

Egypt made you the man who wrote *Bovary* because it crushed your Romantic ideals. You were forced toward Realism. Though the public has given its approval to the shift, I'm trying to understand if it made you happier to see life as a Realist—and become a more successful writer, since I know success was important to you—or if having to turn your back on the Romantic Flaubert was an irreversible downer.

I ask this of myself, and I wonder if I am as romantically attached to some of my own work as you were to *Saint Anthony.* Of all the short stories I've written, two are my "little darlings." One is about a twenty-two-year-old American girl living in a small town in Costa Rica; the details come largely from places I've spent a lot of time. The other takes place in a brothel in Costa Rica, where the prostitutes are all underage boys, not a single American in the story; the details are largely from books I've studied and night drives I've asked my friends to take me on in San José. Are they equally valid? Can you say which story is more real? (We could get into a debate about what "realism" is here, but that's for another letter.) I'll tell you which one excites people more . . . well, I don't have to tell you.

Can something be exotic and real at the same time?

Is the Tourist the romantic and the Traveler the realist? Are we condemned to choose one or the other: grown-up practicality or juvenile wonder? What do we lose when we travel to the land we've mythologized? Even in the end you considered *Saint Anthony* your masterpiece. You published a revised version after *Madame Bovary.* And no one liked it. No one even reads it now. (Sorry.) Apparently, in the case of the work of the great Gustave Flaubert, readers like things concrete, solidly based in a world the writer knows. What does this mean for the "travel writer"—should we stay home, write what we know?

I write you from a desk in Ciudad Colón, Costa Rica. It's been over ten years since I lived here, and I'm still coming back to Costa Rica.

It is now my third day, and I'm staying for a month, living on a compound of artists. They call it a colony. This amuses me, partly because the ants outnumber the artists by a lot.

There are these little ants that I've only known in Central America, and that I'd forgotten about—they are so tiny it took me a while to recognize them as ants—and they have their run of the place. They crawl in and out of our sugar bowls and there's nothing anyone can do about it. For some reason, these ants in Ciudad Colón are crazy for my laptop. They zip between the keys and disappear, then re-appear, seeming to have multiplied. Here's the funny thing about these ants: they know how to play dead. You can flick them, or even squash them with your fingertip, and they will ball up so they look like little black specks of dirt. They'll wait until they think you've forgotten about them, then suddenly unfurl and start crawling as if nothing has happened. I can't shake these ants. I suppose I'll get used to them again.

My desk faces a ten-foot window, and the compound is in a modest rainforest. Nothing fancy, no monkeys or sloths or anything. Occasionally you'll see a toucan. I watch butterflies and birds sucking flowers and pulling worms and hanging in the air. Right now I am watching a yellow bird with a brown back and a black head with stripes like the flames they paint on helmets. I also look out on flowers, birds of paradise that I've only lately seen in flower shops. It startles me to see them half-mast on stalks, growing next to each other non-chalantly, as if they weren't worth seven dollars a stalk.

Here's what I think: you need to leave and then go back to the places that obsess you. If you want the delight of the unfamiliar you leave yourself enough time between trips to activate the added kick of nostalgia when you return. That is what it means to be a traveler: the desire to immerse yourself, for the ants and the flowers and the sticky heat and the language to become "normal"—but always, in the end, to go home, always with the knowledge (or hope) that the future holds another journey like this.

But if you want the delight of belonging somewhere, you have to stay. At some point, you cease being the traveler; at some point you *go native*.

My friend Dave did that. He began as director of the program for which I volunteered all those years ago, and he never left Costa Rica. He works for a Latin American company, the only gringo in the San José office. Karina, his wife, works as a magazine editor in San José. It just so happens that Dave and Karina, now the parents of two boys, live down the hill from the colony in Ciudad Colón, so I've seen them quite a bit. They reside on a compound with members of Karina's family and speak only Spanish to each other.

When I need a break from the colony, Dave picks me up and drives me to the grocery store or back to his home, where he cooks up something amazing.

Ben, Dave and Karina's older son, speaks English with a Spanish accent. He has a mop of light brown hair, but he's a tico.

My Spanish is not what it used to be. It's gotten warped with Cuban slang, and I don't use it enough; it's halting and creaky. I sit at their table and converse with some effort. Monkeys sometimes swing through the trees outside the kitchen window. Rain falls into the open courtyard of their home. This is Dave's idea of normal. Nothing about these things gives Dave the buzz that they give me.

I don't think that's what you wanted, to feel the native.

It was never really what I wanted, either.

You may have been a cocky bastard, but as you got older, you gained perspective. You knew that even though you immortalized Kuchuk Hanem and fantasized that you'd changed her life by visiting her bed, you wrote later that you were nothing to her, and now you knew it. You settled down, in your way. You married yourself to hard work and style, sweating endlessly over one page or the mot juste. And I admire the fact that you went to Egypt at all, when it was such an unusual thing to do, and admittedly involved real physical suffering. Even the fact that you risked (and cultivated) disease, which I never do . . . you *traveler*, you.

May wherever you landed after death offer you a perpetual state of shock and wonder. I'll always imagine the day we might meet. I will continue to indulge in the fantasy of the trips we might take together, perhaps a trip farther down the Nile where it has stayed wild . . . nights of great conversation over absinthe, dipping our pens in ink, rolling cigarettes, reading aloud passages from books, kicking our shoes off in opium dens, and laughing harder than you did with Kuchuk Hanem . . . because our shared laughter would be genuine.

The fact that you are dead keeps my fantasy intact, and I like it that way. In reality, of course, we might not get along at all. But I'll never have to know.

With genuine fondness,
Alden Jones

AFTERWORD

I could travel alone in the world for only so long. When I got married—and I would only have chosen a traveler as my mate—I would have to start thinking beyond myself.

Three months before my wedding I made one last extended solo trip to Costa Rica. I spent the month of May at the artists' colony in Ciudad Colón, and I took a weekend to go back to La Victoria, where I had not been in over a decade. I descended the bus and faced the familiar roadside *pulpería*; the long, skinny government housing where some of my students had lived; and a short way down the road, the school where I had taught. The highway was free of commuters save for a teenaged boy, arms dark with tattoos, huffing up the big hill from Juan Viñas on a child's bicycle. It was one of my third graders, Jesús.

Jesús gave me a surly look. I remembered that look.

"Jesús?" I asked. He broke into a boyish smile.

"You remember me?" he said, puffing.

Jesús dismounted and walked me down to the school. Over the hour the townspeople gathered to greet me. Many of the "chiquitos," now in their late teens and early twenties, were parents. When the bus from Juan Viñas stopped to let off the high school students, Berta Elena descended in her blue school uniform. The wiry, smiling child who once sucked coffee out of a bottle was now a poised almost-adult.

"La Teacher! I cannot believe my eyes!" she said. Berta Elena and I walked to her home, the house where I had lived, and sat with her mother and brother, five-year-old Enrique. Damaris had a look of peace and contentment with the boy at her side; she had told me many times that she wanted another child.

"And Karol?" I asked of her other daughter.

Damaris stared off at the wall.

"In Limón," Berta Elena said. "Working in the banana plantations."

"She is a bad girl," Damaris said.

"She has a baby, a little girl," Berta Elena said, and showed me a picture of Karol, standing next to a skinny, dark man with a baby in her arms, the same giddy smile on her face I used to know.

"He's Nica," Berta Elena said, pointing at the father of Karol's child. Rafael probably had quite a few opinions about that, I thought, but he wasn't home to confirm them.

My old friend Ana was in her tiny cement house, her twin girls toddling outside under the clothesline, her eyes more tired than they once were, but otherwise the same Ana. She was remarried to a good man, but Jason, now seventeen, had renounced her and become an evangelical convert.

"Life is unpredictable, no, Teacher?" she said. "Jason won't even visit me because I don't believe in his version of Jesús. And now look at Rafael, after all his evangelical ways. He's having an affair with an ugly woman in Juan Viñas. I bet he's with her right now!" My jaw dropped. Ana clapped her hands and laughed.

Life was full of surprises. Who on our Semester at Sea voyage would have predicted that three years later Kate and I would wed on a beach in Cape Cod? Abby Vieira, the wife of the Semester at Sea executive dean, presided over our ceremony and spoke about the sea.

At cocktail hour, an oysterman shucked oysters from a dinghy he dragged up from the beach and the bartender served up vodka drinks with fresh mint pressed into ice. Cuban music played in a boathouse where the sails still hung from the rafters.

Now I traveled as part of a team. Funding travel wasn't as easy as it used to be: the economy had tanked, and the jobs I'd counted on to carry me abroad had grown scarce. But there were frequent flier miles, and there was always a way. Kate took me to the places she loved in Guatemala. We hiked and boated around Lago Atitlán, purified our bodies in a sweat lodge, and celebrated New Year's Eve with the expats in Antigua, watching fireworks from the cobblestone square. A few months later we were in the Dominican Republic, the farthest we could get on our miles in the shortest amount of time, at an eco-lodge my sister discovered in *Budget Traveler*. We luxuriated in our thatched-roof hut, read books in hammocks, took long walks on the beach, and dined on lime-seasoned fish and warm tortillas. We got no-nonsense massages that involved mineral-rich mud we then washed out of our hair in the outdoor shower. We attended yoga classes at the beachside studio and walked the meditation path, where images of Buddha were burned onto slabs of rock.

Time was short. Our teaching vacation schedules—I remained in the ivory tower while Kate taught in the public school system— overlapped during Christmas break and six weeks in the summer. I worried less about whether I was a tourist or a traveler, now. I worried about maximizing our time.

In Italy, Kate and I hiked from town to town in Cinque Terre, up jagged stone steps, on cliff paths along the Ligurian Sea, and rented an apartment with no frills but a balcony with a view to kill for. We carried our baby, Gray, on our backs. He was six months old, not yet crawling, perfect for a ride in the Ergo baby backpack. We hiked from one town to the next, stopping in the mornings for frothy cappuccinos, in the afternoons for tomato and mozzarella, prosciutto and melon, pecorino and fig jam, and white wine. Kate, the strong wife, did most of the carrying, and I nursed Gray under a black bandanna, the same all-purpose travel item I'd carried all my life. By the time we arrived in Tuscany, where we paid half price for a spa hotel that was under construction, Gray had learned how to prop himself up on all fours, propel his weight forward, and crawl.

I gave birth to a kid who needs to be on the move. He'll go stir crazy if you keep him inside. As soon as he could walk, he could climb. He's a little Houdini who climbs out of stroller straps and Pack 'n Plays. But put him in an Ergo and offer him a moving view of the Ligurian Sea and he couldn't be more content.

No, there will be no more Cambodia or India for a while. But this gang is on the move.

As for the question of the right or wrong way to travel, it's one I have decided to temporarily defer. Because I know the answer: There *is* a right and wrong way, and sometimes I will do it, and have done it, the wrong way. I might even take my child on a Disney Cruise someday—I'll do anything to entertain my boy, things I never thought I'd do. I hear kids love these cruises, and that adults can even relax knowing their kids are contained—and worse, I might actually enjoy it.

But someday I will be back on a concrete floor, sleeping on a blow-up mattress. I will somehow get back to India. And I will go to South Africa, and Iceland, and Thailand. I will instill in my child a love for the unfamiliar; I will struggle to understand a language and a culture, suffer just enough, teach my students the manners of cultural courtesy.

And sometimes I will let myself off the hook; I will take a pause from judging all by what it signifies and give myself permission to enjoy the Perfect Moment of gazing at the Ligurian Sea past the faces of my wife and child, sipping a hot, milky-sweet cappuccino dusted with cinnamon, the heat of the sun on my skin.

Acknowledgments

This book would not exist without Jason Wilson, champion of contemporary travel writing. Thank you, Jason, my shepherd.

Along my travels my deepest gratitude has been owed to Jeffrey Shumlin, Peter Shumlin, Tim Weed, and everyone at Putney Student Travel. Also: Aaron Levine, Darwin Martínez, Sandra Vigil Conseca, Kate Strickland, David McCrea, Karina Salguero, José Quiros, Doña Martha, Fil Hearn, Semester at Sea, the citizens of La Victoria de Juan Viñas. All my Putney students, the Putney gang, the Cuba crew, the WorldTeach posse: you are some of the best people on the planet.

Thank you to my teachers: Edwidge Danticat, Maria Flook, Douglas Bauer, Rick Moody, Amy Hempel, Russell Banks, Ted Conover. When it mattered the most: Robin Reagler and Margaret Fraser.

And to my readers: Jaime Clarke, Valerie Stivers, Randi Triant, Ricco Siasoco, Andrea Graham, Oona Patrick, David Taylor, Sarah Foy, Kyle Minor, Emily Rapp, Kerry Cohen, Tim Weed, Susan Jones, Lesléa Newman, and Aram Jibilian.

I am indebted to Raphael Kadushin, senior acquisitions editor at the University of Wisconsin Press, and editors Jason Wilson, Oona Patrick, James Hall, and Bill Bryson, who helped portions of this book find print. Thank you to everyone at the University of Wisconsin Press who made the production of this book such a positive experience.

For their incredible support: Amy Jones, John Skoyles, Jomar Statkun, Dana Sachs, the Bennington Writing Seminars, the NYU Creative Writing Program, the Vermont Studio Center, the Julia and David White Artists' Colony, the Bread Loaf Writers' Conference, Chris Castellani and Grub Street, and Emerson College.

Thank you to Kate Bonsignore for providing me with the perfect final chapter in all possible ways.

And to my parents, Susan Jones and Rees Jones, for everything.

References in *The Blind Masseuse* have been made to the following works.

Flaubert, Gustave. *Flaubert in Egypt: A Sensibility on Tour.* Translated and edited with an introduction by Francis Steegmuller. New York: Penguin Books, 1972.

Sontag, Susan. *On Photography.* New York: Farrar, Straus and Giroux, 1977.

Todorov, Tzvetan. *On Human Diversity: Nationalism, Racism, and Exoticism in French Thought.* Cambridge, MA: Harvard University Press, 1993.